Published by Akashic Books
©2018 Justine Bateman

ISBN: 978-1-61775-660-3
Library of Congress Control Number: 2018931219

First printing

Akashic Books
Brooklyn, New York, USA
Ballydehob, Co. Cork, Ireland
Twitter: @AkashicBooks
Facebook: AkashicBooks
E-mail: info@akashicbooks.com
Website: www.akashicbooks.com

FAME
THE HIJACKING OF R

JUSTINE BATEMA

BROOKLYN, NEW YORK, USA
BALLYDEHOB, CO. CORK, IRELAND

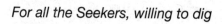

For all the Seekers, willing to dig

TORNADO

Hey, you want to go somewhere with me? I'm talking about emotional time travel. You up for it? I want to show you the inside of something, of Fame, and the only way is for me to pull you in there with me. So, it's me talking. We're going to go in there and I'm going to tell you how it feels. Sometimes I'm talking to you in this book and sometimes I'm talking to someone who took a shit on me in the press or online. I don't want you to take it personally. I'm going to trust you, when I pull you into this emotional tornado. I'm going to trust you to know when I'm talking to you and when I'm talking to not-you. To know the difference. To know if I'm talking to a friendly supporter, a person innocently curious about what Fame is like, or if I'm talking to a malicious hater from my own memory. Just be in there with me. Let it toss you about.

OK. Get in the rowboat and let's go down the river.

MEMOIRS

I fucking hate memoirs. I'm never going to write one. If you thought this was a memoir, put it back on the shelf, or get a refund, send it back. This isn't a shitty memoir. This book is about Fame. It's everything I can remember about being very famous, not so famous, and almost not-famous. It's about all the theories I've drawn about Fame. It's also about society. Why we do the things we do when we're face to face with Fame. I hate memoirs because I hate that *anybody* can write a memoir. You don't have to have any talent whatsoever as a writer or to have particularly good insights; just put down your life, the things you remember about your life. Everyone's got one, a life story to tell. You don't even have to have lived an extraordinary life, just something, anything. You had a pulse for 47 years and then you wrote your "memoir." And I'm not talking about books about unique experiences like surviving a plane crash in the Alps or having been kidnapped. Those books can be compelling. I'm talking about the expanded-Wikipedia-entry books. First of all, most people under 98 years old have no business writing a memoir. They just haven't lived enough of a life yet. They haven't lived enough of a life yet to really craft a proper dramatic arc of it. And, honestly, if your life is interesting enough to write a memoir at 98 years old, then don't bother. Just die and someone will write a biography about you. You will have been *that* interesting a person.

No, I hate memoirs. I'm going out on a limb here, telling you this, because I have a few close friends who have written memoirs. Good, talented people. I hope they don't take offense. There are other people who have written memoirs; people whom I don't know but whom I respect. They may take offense and now never want to meet me because I said I hate memoirs. My friend Marcus mentioned some memoirs he's read that were good; real literary gems. I haven't read them. There are a lot of books I haven't read. So, sure, probably hundreds of these gems exist, memoirs that will blow your mind. I'm sure someone will tell the world all about them, when they leave their critical review for this book online later: "Justine Bateman opens her book with an ignorant rant about the memoir genre." Something like that. That's OK.

I talked with a fair amount of book agents before finding the right one to represent me. Almost all of them wanted me to write a memoir, and not the book about Fame. Hey, maybe they thought I had lived a fascinating enough life for that, or maybe they just felt it was an easy sell. The book agent I finally really connected with never mentioned the word "memoir."

He just loved my writing, the subject matter of Fame, and said, "Let's go." He's also Noam Chomsky's agent. The American intellect and national treasure, Noam Chomsky. If Noam Chomsky's book agent isn't interested in this being a memoir, then no one else should be.

Even one of the publishers I met with, a big publisher, who I assumed was fascinated by the Fame subject matter because they had been anxious to set up a meeting, eventually hit me with, "Wouldn't you rather write a memoir?"

Me, in their office, having just talked about Fame, the sociological theories, my theories, my experience, the experiences of other famous people I'd interviewed. Me, then announcing, "Just so you know, I'm not interested in writing any kind of memoir." They looked at me, eyebrows raised in that maybe-you-didn't-mean-that-aren't-we-still-having-a-good-meeting kind of way. They half blurted out, "Well, don't look around this room!"

It was only then that I actually did look around the office, and noticed that the shelves were lined with memoirs. You name the person, this company has published their memoir.

"Wouldn't you rather write a memoir?"

Aw, you too?

What I *did* get out of that meeting, though, was a completely new direction for the book. Still about Fame (and not a goddamn memoir), but instead of the academic version I had already half-completed, rather a cut-to-the-bone, emotional-river-of-Fame book. (One that my current publisher loves, natch.)

SHEATH

There's this moment I keep flashing on. This scene.
I'm on a couch, in a room. Closed French doors in
front of me. I'm in Miami. At a friend's place? A hotel? I don't know. It's in the early '90s, I think. '92, say.
I'm sitting there. I'm alone. And I feel utterly lost as
to how to handle people coming up to me, recogniz-
ing me. I had been solidly famous for a while. I was
very famous. Can't-go-anywhere-without-people-
reacting famous. So, I'd had people coming up to me
for a while. For a while. What was the fucking problem? Hadn't I had enough practice? Hadn't all those
years of people coming up to me done it? Where
was my resulting proficiency? Why wasn't I a pro
at this now? I still, STILL did not have some reliable
way to deal with the public. I so badly wanted some
dependable blanket-manner to lean on when people came up. It just never came. I was on edge, on
guard, on. Antennae up, all senses pumping, looking, watching, waiting, primed, tense. How's it going
to come at me? It's going to come at me. At what
moment? What person, I mean what kind of person?
A man. A dad? Wants an autograph for his daughter.
So that's it, but then a curveball: he tries to flirt with

me when I hand the paper back. Me, shift gears, pull back the smile, cut that shit off. He's pushed into the aren't-we-having-a-nice-moment-thinking-about-your-daughter and "What's her name?" Me, writing, *Cheryl, All the best, Justine Bateman,* and handing it to him. He slips into that door that's wide open now, no suspicion necessary. The door's not just ajar or half-open with a foot wedged behind the back of it to limit it, but wide open. The daughter, right? Writing something for the daughter.

Then, "I read that you don't wear underwear."

Yeah. Yeah. Y.E.A.H. Yeah, I remember that *Playboy* magazine interview. I said that. I said that. Oh shit, should I have said that? Surprised at seeing my interview verbatim, a fucking relief that I was finally seeing my words verbatim after years and pages and issues and interview after interview of having my words twisted or made up and shoved in my mouth so I sit there in print with the writer's ripped and bloody assessment of me or "angle," or whatever the fuck, spilling out of my mouth as if I had ever said any of that fucking shit or in that stupid way. Yeah, I remember that interview. Panty lines. Pantyhose under jeans on camera so there'd be no panty lines. That's what I said. THAT'S WHAT I SAID, YOU FUCK.

So, yeah. Here's the autograph for your daughter. The one who's, how old is she? Eight, maybe? Nine? Here's that autograph. And you read *Playboy* and you want me? Or you just wanted to say that, or

you just wanted me to know you read my interviews?
Which is it?

You go. You move on and I don't know how the
next person is going to come up to me. Soon. Soon,
someone else will come up to me and I don't know
how. I don't know what they are going to bring to the
plate. I don't know.

I started this book because I was thinking about how
Fame is a mercurial, ephemeral energy, this thing,
this smoke, this cloud. This thing that will make everyone in a restaurant stop being themselves, sit differently in their chairs for the whole time the celebrity
stays in the room there. Talk differently now to their
friend or business associate across the table.

"I CANNOT STOP THINKING ABOUT THE FACT
THAT SO-AND-SO IS SITTING RIGHT OVER THERE.
SO CLOSE. RIGHT over there."

"I remember when I saw that film they were in /
that song they wrote / that home run they hit."

"Oh fuck! People are going to freak when I tell
them who I had dinner with. I mean, I could have
touched them. That close. I brushed past them on
my way to the bathroom!"

"I'll just make it look like I'm checking my e-mail.
Just hold my phone up a bit. Got the shot. Shit, kind
of blurry. Do it again. If I hold it up a little higher, I can
get my face in it too. Oh, that's too good! Yeah, get
my face in there too, hold the phone up just a little

higher. Jesus, I got it. Hold on. Just a minute. I just
gotta post this. Oh shit. Gotta post this to my Facebook. Holy shit. OK. OK. What were you saying . . . ?
Sorry, you know, when will I ever get the chance, you
know? They're sitting right the fuck THERE!"

So, I was thinking about this, how it's not even a
real thing. Fame. Just this thing that society wants to
have. For what? I wanted to cut it open and spread it
out, grab a fork and get in it. Get the wisdom. Understand society's need, the public's need. So, I started.
No big deal. Started writing. Really good academic
stuff. But, I had a shipping container full of FEEL-
INGS about it all. Fuck Fuck. FUCK. This was just
supposed to be an exploration of the Phenomenon
of Fame. Easy. Work, but easy. Not emotional, not
some exploration of my own fucking feelings about
me, about my Fame, about my current lack of it, relatively speaking. Fuck. But, no going back. Couldn't
pull out. Process them. Press those feelings through
the colander. So, OK. My experiences, yeah. I'll tell
you what that was like: The Lifecycle of Fame. The
Beginning, the Love, the Hate, the Equilibrium, the
Slide, the Descent, the Without.

Fame. This thing that came upon me. I didn't have
it and then it was on me. I was without it, nowhere
near it, not cultivating it, not looking for it, knew no
one who had it, just unfamiliar with it, and then it was
on me, enveloping me, encasing me in a sheath that
I could look out of and see the world as I knew it

before the Fame happened, but a sheath that now obscured anyone's vision of me. Can you see me? You see the Fame. Can you ever not see that? Can you ever go back to seeing me without the sheath?

You know I'm not just talking about me, right? I mean any famous person. Can you see them? Like you can see the guy in front of you in line at the drugstore?

"Yeah, he's cute. I wonder if he has a girlfriend. Where is he from? His shoes are nice, probably has money, a career. Is he from here? Maybe he's just passing through. He's not on his phone, poking at it like everyone else in line. That's weird." And on and on and on. You're curious; you wonder. You think about that person, what kind of life that person has, based on the few clues you have in front of you. You make some assumptions. Now, cut to you having seen that person in a movie. He's famous. Now what's going on? Does your heart start pumping faster? Yeah. Why? It's like when you see a guy in school you have a crush on.

"Oh my God, he's walking this way, he must have changed his class order, 'cause I never see him walking down this hall before lunch. Oh God, he is IT . . ." Heart rate elevated. Pupils dilated.

You fight it, maybe even with this guy, this famous guy in front of you at the drugstore. "He's just a person. Just a guy. Calm down. You are not going to ask for a picture. No. No. No. Be cool." But, you are freaking out inside. WHAT THE FUCK IS GOING ON?

OK. OK. Your heart rate escalates in the hall of your school because you like that guy, you want to be with him, you like how you feel around him; it feels good. But, the actor in front of you at the drugstore? Perhaps it's similar, that you want to be with him, even though you know nothing about him beyond the characters he's played. Still, maybe. But what about when you feel that same way when it's an actress? Or an older actor, or anyone famous? Anyone at all. Now our comparison with your crush in the hall at school falls flat. You don't want romantic relationships with *these* famous people. But you suddenly do not entirely feel yourself in line at the drugstore because someone encased in a sheath of Fame is standing in front of you. You are reacting to the Fame. I don't know what that is, that way it makes people freak out, or the way it makes their heart beat faster, or makes them divest themselves of their own personality when they're in front of Fame. Maybe by the end of this book we'll have a robust way to explain it, but for now, let's just say it's magic.

2000

I noticed around 2000, there was this seismic shift in the focus on Fame. There were, by then, many more print outlets, TV outlets, cable outlets that needed entertainment-based material. They'd painted themselves into a corner even, maybe, with the volume of material they needed. Pages and pages and hours and hours of material. The paparazzi population exploded. They were everywhere and they were anyone. Anyone could be in on it.

Actor and "forever brother" Michael J. Fox aptly puts it this way: "It's like your neighbor down the street runs a media empire now." Everybody is generating "content," and much of it is focused on celebrities. They have their "media channels": their Twitter, Facebook, Snapchat accounts with the "potential to reach outside your sphere." That used to be almost nonexistent. There used to be just a few media outlets and just a few paparazzi. Ron Galella once asked, on the slopes of Aspen, years ago, if he could take my picture. I said no and he didn't. Respect. And Roger (how do I not know your last name?), who was at every publicity event in his large, square glasses, low on his nose, with his multitude of cameras slung around his neck, over his shoulder, across his chest. Always there, early at those fake birthday parties *Teen Beat* and *Tiger Beat* magazines used to put together with all the teen stars at the time. Later, at premieres, at openings. Roger, so sweet, who used to bring me slides. No Internet, no WireImage.com to later look up the photos, to feverishly look up photos of yourself a few hours after the event. Roger used to bring slides to events, photos he took of me at the previous event. Roger, who I last saw in a booth at the Silver Spoon coffee shop on Santa Monica Boulevard, hunkered down in a semicircle with a gaggle of other old-school paparazzi. Roger. So sweet.

Pages and pages and hours and hours need to be filled. Many more paparazzi needed. Not just event photos now, but photos of celebrities everywhere, doing anything. And more celebrities. The reality show contestants. Sure, call them "celebrities." Andy Warhol moments. We need them for the pages and the hours. Mike Fox told me that "the biggest prima donnas, the biggest pricks" he'd encountered at any red carpet event were always the reality show contestants. The conclusion being that when you have no discernable skills, you will have cultivated none of the tools you need to handle a public position. That there will have been no means by which you have paid your dues and worked your way—with your artistic craft—up through the ranks to a particular level in your profession, where perhaps Fame is bestowed upon you. If you are absent the work it takes to peck your way out of the eggshell, you will be absent the strength it takes to live outside of that eggshell.

So, yeah. Those who have had Fame placed on them because of skills and talents have a dismissive disdain for those who chased Fame through sensationalism and/or reality-show-contestant debauchery. It's true. Honestly, reality shows are the cancer of America. Look at the current presidency. Oh fuck, I don't want to argue over politics right now. We can get on Twitter for that. Find me at @JustineBateman and we'll take it on. But truly, reality show mentality has diseased this country. Being paid for breathing, bringing nothing to the table, exerting minimum effort at hard work or skill development. Yeah, that's what reality programming gave to our country. Living shit. We had that perfect storm around 2000. Reality shows were gaining traction around the same time that all these entertainment outlets needed more material. Match made in heaven. You also had society wanting to increase the odds of becoming famous, to make new opportunities. Hence, the increased popularity of reality shows. More "celebrities" means more material for the outlets. So, Heidi Montag, The Situation, and so on. I'm sure they're fine people, but who are they?

* * *

An 18th-century satirist named Hugh Henry Brackenridge had a great take on why people without discernable skills and talents are raised up in society
and given Fame. In *Modern Chivalry*, he talked about
politicians and why some of the unqualified ones are
lifted up by the voters. He mentioned this "power of
creation" feeling that courses through people. That
they can feel like God, even, if they lift someone up
and make them famous. Look, what kind of "creating
power" do we have if we merely notice that someone
talented should have attention, should attain Fame?
All we're doing is noticing that. We are not then re-
warded for having a general observation of the obvious. But if we lift someone up to the heights of Fame,
someone who really wasn't that good, wasn't that
talented, wasn't that skilled, well, that's all US; *we*
did that. Not that person's talent, not their skill, not
some manifest destiny of Fame that some person's
skills makes obvious. No ma'am, that was all us. We
can point to that famous person and say, "WE DID
THAT." In that sense, Brackenridge reasoned, in that
sense, we can feel like God.

It's like a Chutes and Ladders board game of
Fame. That's what we've set up in our society. Land
on the right square, make the right move, walk the
right amount of steps, and you will climb the ladder
to a higher position, to Fame. Make the wrong move,
step on the wrong square, and you take the slide
way, way down, away from Fame. We set that up, as

a society. We set that up and we built that scaffolding that sits underneath, those pylons and wood beams in the ocean, under the pier. We built that, together. We watch the 24 hours of "entertainment programming" on E! We buy *InStyle* and *Entertainment Weekly* and *Premiere* and *US* and *People* and *OK!* and *In Touch Weekly* and *Life & Style*. We watch *Entertainment Tonight* and *Access Hollywood* and talk shows in the night and in the day. We read gossip blogs and pass around TMZ videos. We stuff our faces with paparazzi photos of the famous, in line at the grocery store, consuming it, can't get enough of it. Every day.

Now, what's that about? Why is that structure, that support mechanism for Fame, kept so healthy, strong, and robust? We keep it healthy and strong and fed so we can maybe use it someday. "Me!" If you let it die, this support under Fame, you stop feeding it and it will no longer be there for you. If you don't attend to the nail-in-the-wood maintenance of it, of the beams in the water under the pier, it will collapse, and that option for you will utterly disappear. So, we keep it healthy. We read the magazines and watch the shows, and buy the clothes and cars that the famous wear and drive. We create reality programming, even, to make this Chutes and Ladders board even wider. Bigger! More squares! More ladders! Hell, more slides! EVERYBODY CAN BE FAMOUS. More ladders = more lottery ticket buyers. More chances to WIN! We keep it healthy, this machine, because someday, just maybe (we hold the hope), someday we might step on that square that holds the bottom of that Fame ladder and we will fly up it to another plane, another life, a way out of this one, and we will be hovering above, with a bundle of nice stuff.

Prior to the late 1990s, there was no frenzy to be famous. There were those who were tremendously famous, sure, but as huge as the Fame was, it was not coveted by everyone you met. What I mean is, it was compartmentalized, it was thought of with a proper kind of perspective. People were amazed when they saw the famous, but they didn't then immediately after start thinking about how they, too, could attain some Fame. People didn't really think that way back then. You were an actor and you were very famous, but these other people, they had their own lives and their professions and there was a self-respect in that. People seemed to take pride in whatever they were good at, whatever profession they had tackled. A dentist, a publicist, a finance executive, a stationery store owner, whatever. There was not this obsession we have now with becoming famous. There was not this shame that people seem to absorb now, that they or their business isn't "famous." "Gotta make my mark," and not by being a good stationery store owner or a pet store manager, but by getting followers, fans, viewers.

That pride from before faded away for many, and

instead having a camera follow someone around on a reality show started to become a baseline of "approval" and professional self-respect. If a camera was following you around, recording your every banal move, well then, you must really be something. So, around 2000, we had a perfect storm of entertainment-focused shows and magazines needing material, and reality programming making it possible for those lacking entertaining talents to become famous. When social media dropped in, around 2006, then *everybody* could join in on trying to have a semblance of Fame, depending on how many "followers" you had. How many people would be alerted as to where you ate lunch or would see pictures of your dog, wet and shriveled in your sink, while you gave him a bath? How many people? It was at that moment that the dormant human trait of "lack-of-followers paranoia" was awakened.

"I have 315 Facebook followers. Pretty nice. Look at that. Dum-da-dum-dum-dum. What's Dave been up to? Let's see. His account . . . Got it . . . What the fuck? 1,245 followers. What? How . . . How does he know that many . . . That can't be real. How does he have that many followers? What the fuck? I gotta . . . Hey, everyone! I'm going for the big 2,000! Will you help me get there?! Tell your friends to give me a follow. Get me to 2,000!" And that's the way that went. You got those posts, right? Those messages? Your friends trying to "break" 500? Trying to get to

1,000? Something like that? Sure. Kinda made you sick, right? I mean, here's this beautiful tool to stay in touch with your people (or this perfectly evil way to market to you, whichever), and they have to go and pollute it with their lack-of-followers paranoia. That sucks.

OK, I can hear someone: "Who the fuck do you think you are, Bateman? You think, you assume, that everyone was just happy as pie in the '80s and '90s while you rolled around on your haystack of Fame and money and privilege and limousines and helicopters to the Super Bowl? FUCK YOU! You think we were just all happy back then, without all that? And how dare you put down our attempts at grabbing a little bit of that with our Twitter followers and our Facebook friends and our YouTube vlogs. You're not the only one, you know. WE WANT ALL OF THAT TOO." I can hear that. But it's proving my point for me. Everyone deserves respect for what they do, and to be fairly compensated for what they're good at, but for 99 percent of the population, it's *not* for being an actor or a world-famous rock star. And that's OK. That's what I'm saying.

SIZE

Let me tell you how it used to be. This is going to sound like I'm 100 years old and telling you about "what it was like in my day, Sonny," but it's not. It was fairly recent. The Fame in the '80s and '90s was the tail end of the "concentrated audience Fame." Imagine a time without cable TV as you know it, where the Big 3 networks rule. NBC, ABC, CBS. Nothing else matters. There are smaller local stations that play game shows, talk shows, and the reruns of the Big 3 shows. You have HBO in there, but it plays movies that were released in theaters a few years ago ("Home Box Office," get it?). CNN has just started (1980) and Showtime comes along in 1983. So, cable is basically one station trying to fill 24 hours with news every day and a couple of channels playing movies you've already seen. The Big 3 networks were where it was at. And you had to watch the shows when they aired. Recording shows on videotape on your VCR was pretty new, and unless you were good with the VCR timer, it was a virtually useless way to catch your favorite show if you were away from your TV that night. No, this was "appointment television." You've heard that term. So, appointment television and no Internet. Yeah, can you imagine? No 500 channels on cable and no Internet. (Whatever would you do with yourself if you were dropped into 1982 right now?)

OK. No Internet, a few cable channels, and video games were super basic; you went to an arcade if you wanted to play video games. It was the Big 3 networks. That was it. The Big 3 and the movie the-aters. So think about it; if you were an actor on a TV show on one of the Big 3, you were IT. People would rush home from work to catch the show that everyone was going to talk about in the office the next day. You miss the show and you are not part of the conversation tomorrow. No watching an episode on your DVR or binging on the whole season later on Netflix. There was none of that. So, people would not miss their favorite show. They would watch it when it aired. That's weird now. I mean now, I don't know what nights or times my favorite shows are on. Do you? My DVR just grabs them or I find them online later. But back then, everyone made sure they were in front of that TV when the shows aired.

Let's do the math. That translated into an aver-age of 26 million people watching any one of the top three or four TV shows during the 1980s. Every single week. Think about this: the top TV show right now has numbers that would have had it cancelled after its first episode had it aired in the '80s. "Ratings" tell you the percentage of people who had your show

on, out of ALL the people who own a TV. The TVs
that are turned on and the TVs that are off that night.
The "share" is the percentage of people, or "house-
holds," who had your show on, out of all the people who were actually watching TV that night. *Family
Ties* had a 32.7 rating at its height, meaning 32.7 percent of all Americans who owned a TV set (practically
every household owned one) had the show on every
week during that period. Maybe there's one person
in front of each TV, maybe there are four. The population in the US then was about 242 million, so that's
about 62 million people watching. Every week. That's
getting close to modern-day Super Bowl numbers,
you see? Look, I don't want to saddle you with a lot
of math, I just want to show you how concentrated
the TV audience was back then. The top shows now:
Modern Family, say, or *The Big Bang Theory*, are
pulling in a 2.3 rating or a 3.4 rating. You got a population here now of 324 million, so that's 7.4 million or
11 million people watching those shows each week,
respectively. These are the *top-rated shows.* Low
numbers. Millions more people watched one night of
a TV show in the '80s than watch an entire season of
some 2017 shows. That's because the audience now
is fractured, all over the place. 500 cable channels,
more TV channels, TV series still being made on the
Big 4 (there are four now), but now also on HBO,
Showtime, A&E, AMC, FX, etc., etc. Movies still in
the theaters, but video games in the home. Lots of

choices. You can't get those big TV ratings numbers anymore unless you are the Super Bowl.

LOVE

So here I am, I'm in it. 16, I'm 16 when it starts, and I'm in it, in the Fame. Didn't see it coming, just in it. People smiling at me. Happy to see me. SO HAPPY to see me. Like a baby or a toddler. Me. Being looked at as if I am the long-awaited child of a couple who thought they couldn't conceive. Looked at as if I can do no wrong. Everything I do, looked at by others with big, glassy eyes, smiles that cannot be drawn down with any of my actions. Applauded for basic tasks, even. Like a toddler dressing herself, feeding herself, walking, running, scribbling shit on a piece of paper with a crayon and up on the refrigerator with PRIDE. Everybody loving you. You, celebrity. You, newly famous person. Everybody loves you. Is proud to throw their arms round you and call you "pal." People who would make a show of snubbing you are now claiming your friendship, hat in hand. Or unconsciously so, like an old coat-check ticket to retrieve a long-ignored coat in the back of the closet there by the maître d'.

"YES, that one. The one I refused when you mentioned it to me weeks ago. NOW, I'll take it. And I'll wear it now, because it's CHANGED."

Yeah, you get those. You get those. You get it all. It will get worse. When you're in a bar and some guy, drunk, wants you, wants to be with you, takes the "control" road and tries to rip you a new one for smoking. Your regular habit, the one you've had since you were 17 in high school, trying it out, getting used to it. Anyway, now, for years, a regular thing, not a change from who you were. But this guy, this guy is on the "control" road of getting at you and says, "Ew, I didn't know Mallory smoked." Trying to be controlling. Like you've disgusted him; he had such high hopes for you, thought so well of you. You had that! You had this guy thinking so highly of you! There it was and there it goes. You just fucked up. You disappointed him, drove him away, this approval, affection that was so freely yours. You blew it.

Yeah. It will get worse, but for now, oh man, the attention is kind of weird, kind of exciting, kind of feels like an accomplishment, acknowledgment for your work. That's what it is, right? OK. Maybe there's some formula here, a correlation. Success = Fame = accomplishment. Just correlation or causation? Whatever, correlation, they're related. You learn this. You're 16. Seems right. They keep rising, your ratings and your Fame. They keep going up, both of them, together.

ANYTHING

There was this photo shoot. Me and actress Sarah Jessica Parker. Me, 18 or 19, Sarah, the same. Photo shoot for *Tiger Beat*. Teen fan magazine. Harmless. Photo shoot with some clothes we had in our closet. That's all.

"What are we doing today?"

"Let's do a photo shoot." Grab some crap in our closets—T-shirts, jeans, NOTHING. Belts, hats, and crap we had bought at army surplus stores. Whatever.

"We want to do a photo shoot." Of course for publication. No question. Never a question/doubt. Wide-open doors. Somehow a photo studio, somehow a photographer, somehow immediately printed in the magazine. No question. Here. Here, for you. Whatever you want. Two teenagers with whatever out of their closets; shit you couldn't get rid of at a garage sale. No questions asked, photo shoot and publication provided. Open doors, open smiles, open, open.

Concerts, backstage passes, cops letting you go when pulled over for a ticket (not always, but half the time), Super Bowl game. Super Bowl XXI, maybe XXII, I don't know. Hosting MTV's halftime show.

Limo pickup, always a limo pickup, then in a helicopter. A helicopter because of the traffic. Skip the
traffic, fly over the traffic. Let down anywhere. On
the grass right there, in front of the stadium. It's the
Super Bowl, we have celebrities in the helicopter,
we land wherever we want. Usher you in. Here
are your free tickets, your free impossible-to-get,
only-for-sponsoring-entities, 50-yard-line, you-
made-not-one-effort-to-get-these-tickets Super
Bowl tickets. Sure, you'll host the halftime show
later in a room where you cannot hear yourself talk
into the mic because of the screaming, the cheering,
the volume. But man, you don't give a shit. THIS IS
AWESOME. Like sitting in in an effortless, delicious
orange custard cloud of favor all the fucking time.
All the time. Everyone wants you, to be with you, be
near you, give you things, do you favors, LISTENING
INTENTLY TO EVERYTHING YOU ARE SAYING.

Yeah, that was a big one. Everyone was listening intently to what I was saying. A circle of people.
Around me. Adults. Me, a teenager, or early 20s.
Done nothing, really. Traveled, OK. Was a good stu-
dent, OK. Showed up to work on time, OK. Worthy?
Worthy of being listened to as if a river of holy wisdom is pouring through my mouth? No. NO. But, the
feeling. Oh, it felt good. At that age, to be heard, to be
taken seriously. Shut up. OK. Listen to the Fame. The
way these people, or why these people, were listening to me so closely. So careful not to bring up any-

thing about themselves and risk ripping my interest from this circle of people. Keep me from wandering off. Keep me there. We love to hear ourselves talk. Best way to keep someone engaged is to ask them about themselves. Keep a celebrity there, let them talk, hear them, REALLY hear them, show you hear them. Nod your head somberly when they make an "interesting" point, laugh quickly and heartily when they say anything amusing. KEEP. THEM. THERE. OK. So, here we had it, I had it, in spades. Spades. Everyone would stop and listen.

You see? You see what happens? The celebrity, the famous person, gets used to this. They get used to it and come to expect it. They have to because it happens all the time, every day. OK, so you expect it and you then stop asking anyone else about themselves. You just forget. It's not part of the exchange anymore. You talk and talk. You pontificate. It seems to be what people want. They want to keep you there, and you, the famous, what are you doing? Why do you keep talking? What are you doing? You are delivering. They need something, this group, this circle of people, and you are reading the group and making an assumption. You're right, your guess is right, and you perform, deliver. You want to make sure you aren't trashing all this goodwill being handed to you. You don't want to be like Justine Bateman when that guy in that bar was so disappointed in her smoking

a cigarette. She trashed all that goodwill, all the adu-
lation he was just handing her. You don't want to be
like that, right? So you give it, you deliver. And you
get used to this performance to such an extent that
you forget to behave any other way. So there's that.

CIRCLE

I'm going to tell you about something that happened the other day. I mean now, you know, present day. I was meeting some new friends, people in the business, and there was this one woman, actress. Well-known, yes, but not overly so. Where am I, on the Fame scale there? I don't know. How famous am I? How do I rank compared to her? I don't know, it doesn't matter. It shouldn't matter, but she's somehow ALIVE. You know? Alive and magnetic and ON. Not in a bad way, in a good way, in a magnetic way—she's just in that zone. And I mention the "where do I rank" question because I found myself doing that leaning-in-and-listening-to-whatever-she-was-saying thing. That thing I told you about a couple of pages ago. I'm doing that thing. We're all oriented around her. I think we are, I can't tell because we're in a circle, you know? Anyway, I don't feel myself. I'm fucking DIVESTING. I feel like I'm "divesting myself in front of Fame." That's why I'm asking myself about the "ranking," the Fame ranking, because I'm trying to reason with myself.

"C'mon. She's not more known than you. You should be able to keep your sense of yourself. This

is easy. WHY ARE YOU NOT FEELING LIKE YOUR-
SELF NOW?" I try to jolt myself back into "being myself" by talking more energetically and loosely when
I see a chance to speak. It doesn't work. I try again. I
try to focus on someone else. Fuck. She's great, this
actress. I like her a lot, but fuck. She has that thing
on her, that sheath. OK, we all did, in that group, to
some extent, sure, but hers was turned ON. It was
plugged in and I felt it. That magic thing. Fucking
weird. We'll figure it out. Maybe by the end. Maybe
on the last page here in this book.

SHIP

This Fame was given, bestowed. Energy that cannot be destroyed, only changed. Not removed, only paused. This Fame must continue for the professional machine to function. Work booked, money paid, commissions paid, by the performer. A business. Fame as the fuel. You've got your team: your agents and managers and publicists. And you fill your support group. Not the work team, but the population of your world: those who will be on this plane of existence with you. There are other famous people who also live on this plane, and then there are people who live in the "real" world who can transition back and forth through that membrane to the Fame plane. They are cool enough, chill enough, don't lose their shit when in front of the famous. They can travel back and forth between the two worlds. They can do it. Not that many. Hold onto those, get them in your group. They make it comfortable. You can "be yourself."

Aw shit. What is that?

Who are you? Are you this famous person? Are you the person you were before the Fame? Or are you something else? OK. How old were you when you became famous? If you became famous later in life, when you were an established, full-grown adult, then I don't know. Maybe you are "you." You know you, you are a fully baked person and then you have this Fame and you being yourself is just this person you were before you became famous. No big deal. Good for you. That sounds clean and easy. Good. I'm talking about—maybe it doesn't matter how old you are when it happens, when Fame gets sprayed all over you like red paint from a PETA demonstrator on Fifth Avenue and you in the fur coat you just pulled out of storage. Red all over the coat. Everyone knows now. You are covered. So, covered with Fame. To be yourself . . . That's . . . what is that? Do you know? Are you too young to have that under your belt yet? NOW YOU ARE FUCKED. How are you supposed to get that?

You were going to learn to be yourself, what that is. You had an idea of the field and the seeds and the watering and all that, and you kind of started on the land there. You tilled the soil of understanding yourself, I guess. But, now you're on a boat. A fucking boat: the Fame, OK? Fuck. I mean, good, here you're going on an adventure, but on a boat. Where are you supposed to farm the land now, to become completely yourself? All those things you need to do, to grow, to cultivate your personality, try your choices, see the results? Shit. You find a pallet, a container, something flat, there on the boat. You find some dirt, maybe you brought a little with you. You pull it out of your pocket. A handful, maybe more. You turn the pocket inside out and get all the dirt from the seams of the coat pocket, scrape it out. You have some seeds, not all the seeds you wanted, but some, they'll grow. Maybe you can get more dirt and more seeds from the islands, the lands you come to in the boat. You make a little plot with the dirt and your seeds and you give the plot its water.

OK, you see? That plot of dirt and seeds and maybe plants, hopefully, somehow, is YOU. That's the real you, trying to grow. Trying to be what that large plot of dirt and land was supposed to be, back home, on the mainland, before you got on this Fame boat. The plot of land all the people living in the "real" world get to use—the time they have there, the support of the land and the groundwater and all that. Not this tiny fucking pallet of dirt, this small container of dirt you have to guard from the elements of the sea and the wind and the fucking seagulls who are so damn excited to have the chance to eat some seeds, to have some food without having to be on land, without having to fly ALL the way over to that island they can barely see in the distance. Like that. OK, that's the real you. You are on a boat, a ship, a huge ship, and you are not the captain. You are not steering this ship. It's the Master of Fame. Captain Fame, and you are just on it, the ship. Each famous person has her own ship. All these famous people, each with their tiny pallet of dirt, "themselves," their true selves, guarded by them from the elements and the wind and fucking seagulls.

You also have some people you can "be yourself with," your group. And if you're young and have this little dirt plot on this ship, you are growing your plants when you're with them, those people who can cross the membrane. That's how much time you have to do that. Only when you're with them. Because when you're alone, you are battling. You're battling the doubts, the criticisms. You're reviewing. You're reviewing everything you've done.

Was I rude to those people when I said I didn't want to take a picture with them? Shit, was I rude?

Aw, your mom or your dad said you were rude and "Why couldn't you have just taken a picture with them? Would that have been so difficult?"

SHUT THE FUCK UP. Do you have any idea how many fucking times people want my picture, want my autograph, want to have me, stand next to me? Stop, stop. C'mon, not your parents.

Yes, from their perspective, from sitting outside it, from seeing it just a few times a month, seeing you a few times a month in the crush of the public, to them it seems like no big deal; the refusal of the pictures, the autographs looking rude, uncaring, ungrateful even. They don't know the crush. They see a small . . . They don't know, don't mean it. They're just adding another straw to the haystack of criticism of your behavior.

So, you think, you review. You aren't often prac-

ticing being the real you. You can't. You are when
you're with those people, though. You've populated
your world where the planting the seeds and the
growing the plants can happen with no threat of wind
or waves or those fucking seagulls. They're there,
those people. I had them. It was important to have
them. Kelly and Billy B. and Howard and New York
Fucking City. Leif and Scott and Jonesy and Nina and
bean oil burning in Michael Bowen's Indian motorcy-
cle, riding behind that, in the 2nd Street Tunnel, to
the clubs in downtown LA. Those people. Those people who are on the plane or who can pass through the
membrane between the "real" world and this plane
of existence you have to live on. The ones who will
close in around you when they sense the shit is coming down, when they sense the infiltrators are trying to make a move. They get you away from them,
get you out the back door, get you to a better place.
Those guardians of the universe. Those people. SOLID
FUCKING GOLD PEOPLE.

And you become yourself. You grow that plot. It's
not the same as the big plot, the solid in-the-ground
plot you would have had back on the mainland, had
you never gotten on this boat, this ship, but it's good.
You kinda get there OK—with different, exotic seeds,
to boot. You've gotten them from distant lands, new
plants. It's not all bad, that personal development
that had to happen on a little pallet of dirt on a ship
with Captain Fame. It's not so bad.

NOT-A-PERSON

It's a whole other plane of living, Fame. Another plane of existence. A parallel universe laid over this one, the "real" one. Or really just the one most everyone else is on. Is it real? Which one is real? Both of them? You can't get out. No one will let you. You cannot be not-famous. You haven't changed, but everyone, EVERYONE, looks at your sheath. Not you. You are separate. You're separate and you're not real, even. You're not there, even. You're not there. You change everything when you walk into a room, but you're not there. We can talk about you like you're not there, because you're not-a-person. We can rip into you because you're not real. It's like in a film, when you're killing a lifelike robot, a replica. Should we feel bad about it? Morally? Is it morally right to kill a replica if they're not-a-person? Celebrities, same thing. Rip them apart, rip them a new asshole.

"They signed up for this. They asked for this. They wanted this. Well, here's what you get. I hate you. I love you. I want to rip your head off."

I was in an elevator once. An elevator, seven feet by six, something like that, the average size of an elevator. Small. You've been in an elevator. OK, put three people in there. Three people. I'm one of them. The other two are people I don't know. They know each other, they're together. OK. They're talking. They're talking about me. Me.

They say, "Her hair is darker on TV." Me. I'm standing there. If I had reached my arm out, I would touch one of them, close. Talking about me, but I'm not there. I'm a poster? An image on a poster? Or I'm on TV. I'm . . . There's a TV in the elevator and I'm just on it. I'm not really there. Is that it?

"You know I can hear you."

This was after they'd said some other stuff. Can't remember. Some other stuff before they said my hair was darker or lighter, whatever. It's happened before. People looking at me, talking about me, gesturing. Everywhere. Everybody. Thinking I can't see them, hear them. Assuming? Hoping? Assuming I can't see them recognize me, watching me, whispering about me. Assume I can't hear.

So, "You know I can hear you."

I already feel bad, they don't see me, don't want to see me, have shut me out.

YOU'RE OVER THERE AND NOT-A-PERSON. We will ignore you. Make you feel shitty.

OK, I'm already there and, "You know I can hear you."

They look at me slightly shocked, offended. Offended that I spoke? That I interrupted them. That

I dared to interrupt them. Me and my not-a-person status interrupting them. Two friends, two close friends having a discussion about me. DO NOT IN-TERRUPT. Who do you think you are, interrupting us? We who are real and having a real conversation. Goddammit, a private conversation. How dare you. Who are you? You're not even a real person. We will treat you as if you are a joke even. Not-a-real-person and a joke. A monkey who performs for us, but DOES NOT SPEAK. We will give you money and attention and we will watch your shows and pay for theater tickets to your plays and to your movies and we will buy your magazines, the ones you are on the cover of, being-yourself or not-being-yourself, and we will participate in your Fame. We will support it and keep it robust because we need it to stay there, we need it to be real and big and tangible. BUT YOU WILL NOT INTERRUPT THE CONVERSTATIONS OF REAL PEOPLE. You are not real.

"You know I can hear you. I'm right here."

Me almost, under the skin, apoplectic. I can't believe they don't understand the fucking laws of physics or the carry of sound in the air or the fucking proximity of our three bodies.

"I can hear you."

They look at me with small shock, but more of-fense. They are offended. I broke the rule. I shattered the fourth wall. I reached across the membrane be-tween my plane of living and theirs. Out of my world, into the "real" world, and they were offended. I had been . . . rude? I was rude. I was rude for doing that to them. I can't be in their world, their "real" world. Get the fuck out of our world.

A good friend of mine, a wife of a famous actor, told me about a time, one of the many times, that she was seen as not-a-person. Even worse, an obstacle. An obstacle between the fans and her husband, someone to be circumnavigated, or to be used to get to her husband. She told me about one day, late afternoon, a woman with eight teenagers was at her front gate, trying to talk to her son there, on the other side of the gate.

My friend's son, seven years old or so, trying to shoot baskets in his front yard, and this woman crying out to him to "go get your dad. We're here to see your dad." As if he, the son, is also someone to circumnavigate or to use to get to the famous person. "Go get your dad for me." My friend, the boy's mother, she comes out.

"This is a private home. You need to leave right now."

The woman, indignant, INDIGNANT. Outraged at being questioned, at being (possibly) turned away. She wasn't having that. She'd had a fucking plan.

"But, we drove 60 miles! How dare you!" she bellowed at my friend. "How dare you. You're going to deny my kids seeing him?"

Can you stand this? Can you imagine? "WE DROVE 60 MILES." You told these teenagers, perhaps coordinated with their parents, put these teenagers into your car, and drove an hour or more, and then expected, demanded, that this child and this wife produce this famous person. Because they are not-people. Not the boy, not my friend, not the famous actor. None of them.

This happens; this happens a lot. You retreat, then, if you're famous. You have a world, and there's this other world. But, you are shut out. Don't have an opinion.

"Shut up, you fucking actress. You dumb fucking actress." Shut up.

So, you build your world up. You have friends, you make friends. You make a world, you populate your world. People you trust. People you don't trust, but at least treat you as a person. Not as not-a-person. You let them around. Maybe not in, you don't let them in, but you let them around, because with them you are at least not not-a-person. You have good friends, and you have your "team." Your agent, your manager, your publicist, like I mentioned before. You have these. They depend on your Fame, your level of Fame; they make a commission on the work that needs your Fame. The Fame is the fuel, the currency. You pay the publicist to help control the Fame or generate direction, action. You take that Fame and . . . You don't take the Fame; the Fame takes you and you have opportunities because of it. You have work opportunities and everyone is happy and needs the Fame to continue because it is the fuel for the machine. The machine will spit out nothing without the Fame. So, you want to leave? Go and just be a "real" person? You want to take off? No. People have done it. Some people have done it. At the height. Dave Chappelle, Josh Hartnett, Meg Tilly. I've heard of some who left abruptly, out, like that. Gone. And then back, sometimes back. But, the TEAM. Dependencies. Not bad. It's good, They're not bad, the team; there's a purpose. But, the Fame, see? The Fame must continue.

ON

I was at the National Association of Television Program Executives (NATPE) convention in San Francisco. 1986 or '87. There to help *Family Ties* make the sale to the syndication market. Whenever your program was about to hit the 100th episode, the networks would bring all the actors out to this convention to show them off to the local station executives. An enticement for them to buy the reruns of the show. So, there we were: Michael Gross, Meredith Baxter, Mike Fox, Tina Yothers, and me. We're flown out and let loose amongst the syndication executives, to mingle and make conversation at this reception, there in our hotel. This is one of those occasions where you are to turn your Fame ON. You are not bulldozing through a shopping mall or an airport, careful to always keep moving and to avoid eye contact so you don't get pulled down in a mob of handsy autograph seekers. No, this was smiling and greeting and inquiring as to the health of these people's dogs. You were performing; you were Being Famous. This is the mode you entered for "public appearances": parades, awards show presentations, mall openings. (Sure, I did one of those with my brother when we were first, not-quite-famous. They gave us each $500 worth of electronics for it. We were teenagers. It was fabulous.) So, I'm there, ready to smile and greet and ask after their dogs. I was always good at these things, right out of the gate.

Smile, shake hands, laugh at their comments, "Hey, Mallory! Where's Nick?!" and watch them guffaw and slap each other on the backs over their own cleverness. Look, I'm not mocking them. It was just tiresome to hear the same comments from each cluster of people, each person assuming it was the first time I'd ever heard it.

So, I'm talking and smiling and answering their questions and meeting whatever relatives they've brought with them. Their wives, daughters, aunts, cousins. Whoever. They get them passes to come meet the cast of their favorite show. Shaking hands, smiling, listening, talking. Keeping an interested look on my face, smiling, moving onto the next person when it seems like the current person wants to kick the conversation up to the "Why don't you come have dinner with the family tonight?" level. And then suddenly, I'm running on fumes. My Being Famous Performance Gas Tank has just run dry. I told you I was good at this right out of the gate. But, I was never good at keeping it going past a certain point. Maybe an hour, max. Then my tank runs out. The muscles in my face feel shaky from holding the smile for so long. My face feels like it has to choose between staying in this full-smile position or releasing the expression of any emotion at all. The facial muscles don't feel like they can hold anything in between. Frozen full-smile, or nothing. Then my cheeks feel like they're going to spasm from holding the smile and my brain doesn't want to create conversational responses anymore. Doesn't want to talk. Fumes running low now. I have to get out of there. I make some excuse, even though I have two more hours to be there, to smile and to chat, and I hustle to the hotel elevators. I hope no one will try to talk to me on my way.

I say, "I'll be right back, I just have to . . ." Now I'm bulldozing. Let them think I just got my period or something.

Let them elbow each other knowingly, "lady issues" and all that. I don't care. Bulldoze to the elevator. No one in it, thank God. Up to the room. Out on my floor, open my hotel room door, and get on the bed. Just sit on the bed. I just need nothing. Just sit and not talk, not smile, not think, if I can. Just have to do nothing for a while. I don't know how long. Long enough to feel that my face can accomplish a look between manic happiness and apathy. Long enough to feel that my brain will accommodate small talk once again. At first, the time I think I need seems endless. I don't know how long this will take. I just have to wait. But, I know I have to go back down there. And smile and shake hands and be ON. Eventually, I get there.

* * *

One of my favorite sociologists, Erving Goffman, would call this exceeding "the temporal length of performance." His theory being that we are always engaged in "impression management": trying to control what others think of us. He found that we can only spend so much time "playing host" or being nice to people or being ON. Like when you have a house guest, someone you're not particularly close with, you can't have them there in your house for that long, it's too exhausting, too exhausting to be ON for them, to be cordial, up, hospitable. You can only maintain that performance for so long. Then you gotta get them out.

LETTERS

Something that has been flipped onto its head over the last 20 years is the star-fan interaction. I'll paint the picture of this interaction in the 1980s and '90s. Someone likes watching a performer's TV show or film. They watch the show, they watch this performer on talk shows, and they read their magazine interviews; they "follow" them. Then, they want to let this performer know that they like their work.

"Hmm." No Internet. No Twitter accounts. "Hmm. Can't call them on the phone. I'll write a letter!" You think about writing a letter, but you've got to get to work or school. You'll do it later. Well, maybe this weekend.

While you're waiting for some laundry to finish drying a couple of days later, "Hey! I'll write that letter now. Get my stationery out. And an envelope . . . Got it. *Dear Justine, etc., etc., etc.* OK, done. Fold it up, put it in the envelope. Hmm. No stamps. I'll have to get some tomorrow." Three days later, you've got the stamps. Put one on. The address—

"Well, I guess I'll just send it to NBC. Or would Paramount Studios be better? That's where they shoot the show. OK, Paramount Studios address.

Well, it's in Hollywood, California. I guess I could call them to get the address. I could call 411 and get the number to Paramount Studios and then call them to get their address. OK, got it! Phone call made, address on, and next time I pass a mailbox, I'll pop it in. Great!"

Tick-tock. Tick-tock. Mail is processed. It arrives at Paramount Studios! It's sorted and a pile is brought to the production offices for each of the TV shows shot there. That mail is sorted so that each actor gets his letters. A pile is placed in his dressing room. Hooray! And the actor, rehearsing, shooting the episodes, will get to that pile later, to that pile addressed to him. Maybe he will read them and answer them all personally, or he may hand them over to his assistant to read, or to the president of his fan club, or to his mom, because she's been reading his fan mail for him lately and has been sending out pictures with a signature that is authentically forged by her. Or maybe the actor will never open that particular pile because his schedule is too packed to take the time, to think about it.

And that is the journey of a fan letter in the 1980s and '90s. That is the way in which you would reach your favorite performer. A lot of effort on the fan's part, right? I mean, the stationery, the composition of the letter, the stamp, finding the address, getting to the mailbox, all of it. You can see how only the most dedicated fan would bother with all those steps. We can assume that for every 100 people who wanted to say something to their favorite performer, maybe only ten actually got out the stationery. And of those ten, maybe only four get the letter to the mailbox. So, out of all those fans, maybe only four percent are actually sending you anything. And maybe you have read it. Or not.

Today, in 2018, bippity-bop, type *Jessica Chastain's Twitter* into the Google search bar. There it is. Type *@Jess_Chastain I think you're great!* and hit send. Done! Whoa. What just happened? You just sent a message to the award-winning actress Jessica Chastain, and no matter where she is, at home or on location for her next big film, if she's someone who reads her Twitter "replies," oh mama, she just read your note. Whoa. Right in there. Right into her life. What an amazing thing!

So, this new way, this new right-into-your-life way for reaching your favorite performer is nice for the public, and for the performers. But, what if the person has something very nasty to say? Well, in the 1980s and '90s we already know the effort that would have taken to send the glowing fan letter. It was the same for sending vitriol. For every 100 people who were incensed with a famous perfomer, maybe only four percent were sending the letter. Really, it was probably only one percent. Why one percent? Because back then, the mere idea of speaking rudely to another person, let alone an actor you have watched and maybe admired (even though it felt more like dislike at the moment), was uncommon. It just didn't happen that much. There were the letters, sure, from the "We are going to be together forever" senders, the letters you forwarded right to Gavin de Becker and Associates Security, but almost everything else was pleasant. When you have to write a letter, you're automatically put into a state of composure and a kind of formality. You can't help it. So, no, I never once got a letter where someone just popped off at me. No matter how many millions of people watched our show back then, not one poison-dagger letter.

I remember one that took me by surprise, though. I once got a letter that said (I'm paraphrasing), *I have been watching you and I have noticed that your ears stick way out. You should get that fixed.* I was a little stunned. Here are all these letters asking for autographed pictures or saying how the show cheered them up during a sad time in their lives, and this one, this letter, was telling me I needed my ears fixed. I had never before had any thoughts about my ears. I looked in the full-length mirror there in my dressing room. I pressed my ears against my head with my fingertips. Against my head and then let them go. Did it a few times. Yeah, I guess they do stick out. I guess so. But that's where my hair goes when I put it behind my ears. How could my hair fit there if the ears didn't stick out? Me, trying to see the logic behind this comment, until I finally just put the letter away, resigned to not understand what this guy was talking about.

A couple of years later, I got another letter (Yes) saying, *I sent you a letter a few years ago about your ears sticking out. I can see that you have not fixed them yet. And they're a lot worse.*

You might be confused right now or chuckling to yourself at how tame those letters were, in comparison with what is said online to famous performers nowadays. And yet, it took me by surprise back then. In 2018, the way people pop off at famous performers online is eye-wateringly shocking. To talk to anyone like that is stunning, but to say it to someone you have never met, someone who commands respect for putting themselves out there, for being creatively vulnerable every time they make some entertainment for us, is jarring. It's easy to pop off now, though.

Malicious fans have no skin in the game; they're not saying these things to a famous performer's face. They've got no letter to write. They're hiding there behind their "egg" avatar and their "Joined in October 2013" bio information. Maybe for every 100 fans who thought about saying something nasty to singer Justin Bieber this month, maybe 200 did. You see what I did there? Maybe *twice* as many actually did it. Because there's no letter to write, no stamp or address to get, no trip to the mailbox. Just a few keys pressed on the laptop or phone, and "send." Done. *Fuck you* and send. It takes under 30 seconds and then they're back to watching TV or washing their car or pretending to pay attention in their meeting. They are back to it.

Others online see that comment and they start the pile-on.

Yeah! Fuck you, Justin Bieber! Maybe they are part of the 100 who already wanted to give that famous performer a "piece of their mind" or maybe they were part of the second 100, the ones who just like a good pile-on. They just see the chum in the water and want in. They like the rush of it. The famous performer, meanwhile, is now under a hailstorm of shitty online comments, half from those who feel they have a beef with him, and half from those just there for the blood, to watch the blood run. For sport. Yeah. What a shame; they took this beautiful tool to directly reach their favorite performer and they just took a shit on it.

What's that about, even? That extreme love/hate of the famous? Social science philosopher René Girard coined this phrase "mimetic desire" in 1961. He didn't think anyone was born with innate desires for possessions, professional positions, etc. He theorized that those desires are learned, that we simply imitate others' desires. That we observe other people wanting things and then we want them. He also theorized that "metaphysical desire" was where the desired items (things that the other person wants, like things you see a famous person wanting or buying) just represented someone's true desire to actually *become* that person.

You know where I'm going with this. OK, it's obviously not possible to become another person, so that famous person actually becomes the *obstacle* to this desire, this desire to become that famous person. It goes a long way to explaining how someone can simultaneously love and hate a famous performer. They want to buy what that famous person has, dress like they dress, but they also seem to hate them. See? The famous performer, himself, is blocking this person's chance to become him. Pretty interesting shit.

GLOVE

Jesus, there was this one woman at this party. Whenever someone came up . . . Look, I had found this
great way to end a conversation with a fan, someone in public. Someone who was going on and on
and hey, they're just excited, I get it, but going on
with no signs of stopping. How do you get yourself
out of there? Where there's no one to pull you away
or you've committed the first sin of being famous,
which is that you have stopped moving. You're supposed to never, ever stop moving through a crowd.
But, let's say you have stopped, weren't paying attention, and someone has captured you, like a wild
animal. Captured you and now is talking to you and
is amazed that they are talking to you, to this sheath
of Fame. They can't even really see you. OK, talking
to this sheath you're in, and how do you get out of
their grasp? I had this way, this foolproof way of getting gone.

"It's nice *to have met* you" and maybe a handshake.

"It's nice *to have met* you," so I'm putting the
whole encounter in the past tense. See how I did
that? Pretty clever. Worked like a charm. For years.
The fan knew the encounter was over, just followed

the past tense I'd presented, smiled, and moved on. Worked great. I was really, really pleased with myself that I had finally, finally come up with at least a portion of a blanket way to deal with people approaching me. I even passed that along to other famous people.

"Hey! I've discovered a method! Something that . . . a KEY, even, to escaping these situations!" So proud of myself; worked like a charm.

So, I'm at this party recently, a few months ago, Christmastime. At this party, I'm there as a guest, OK? Not "my people," but there as a guest, so be nice, be polite, be conversational, be generous. Be nice. This woman, DRUNK. This woman comes up to me.

"You're Justine Bateman. You're that girl." And so on. It went on and on. I don't remember exactly what she said, I blocked it out. Then, me, wanting to get out of this, wanting to get back to the interesting conversation I'd been having with these two other people before this woman abruptly cut in.

I say, "Well, it's nice *to have met* you."

Oh shit. The look on her face. The look on her face, as if some demon had just put her on like a glove and was now, for the first time, was now going to fucking punish me for having used this method for getting rid of people, for getting rid of ALL those people, in the past. Now this demon with this drunk-woman-glove on was going to let me fucking have it.

"Oh. You're a rude one, aren't you?"

Whoa. I was shocked. Shit. My foolproof, pat-ented-almost, end-of-the-conversation trick was grabbed and refused. Snatched and turned onto a dagger held in this glove. The look on her face, the venom.

Me, shit. Me, "I just want to get back to this con-versation. It was nice *to have talked* to you . . ."

Her, saying something else, something more, wanting to fight, and me, trying to keep it calm, try-ing to be the nice guest-of-someone-else-at-this-party. Yeah, if it had been another setting, another party, me as not-a-guest-of-someone-else, I would have tried a non-AT&T-customer-service response. I would have told her to fuck off. But I was a guest. I was a guest . . . It was a great method while it lasted.

Christ, I've told you a lot of bad or weird stuff about Fame. It is really nice sometimes, when someone comes up and tells you that they like your work. That's really nice. That's the best of it. But, it's not about the Fame, they're not freaking out over your Fame, just telling you they like your work. Especially when they've seen a film you directed at a film festi-val or a play you acted in, because only a few thou-sand people could ever have seen those, only a few thousand total could have filled those seats, and this person took the time to come and watch that film or that play.

Yes, but that's not what we're talking about here in the book. The Fame makes you recognizable so people can see you and maybe they are one of the few thousand who saw a play or someone who was jolted out of a sad time in their lives because you made them laugh on a TV show. That's nice. That's good, but that's not really it, is it? That's . . . I consider that to be "work related." Things attached to the work. I'm talking about the Fame here. The ephemeral quality that I told you about. It's nice, that recognition for your work. I wish that was all Fame was. It used to be, in another era. It seems like it used to be.

CRUSH

There's this thing, this event, this incident I keep wanting to write down, that happened the other day, in the grocery store. I'm not recognized that much anymore, nowadays. Into other things, directing, writing, producing, tech. Different time, very different time. Not acting. Acting was very good to me for a very long time, but I feel that desire has passed, really. Anyway, not recognized that much anymore. Piling my groceries on the cashier conveyor belt. The guy behind me, looking at me with slightly eager eyes. I recognize that, I get it. Make him feel OK with it, comfortable with it, with his own discomfort.

Him, dying to say something, then finally, "I had such a crush on you, before."

Automatic, I think to say, "Well, what happened? Don't you have a crush on me now? What's changed?" I don't say it. Always think to say it, but don't. I think of something else to say, the other automatic thought, "Are you trying to tell me you touched yourself?"

I mean, OK, not fair to him. Yeah. Look, there was a period, I don't know, ten years ago, where at least once a month some guy would come up, or guys in work situations—writer/producers at auditions, maybe—and tell me that I was the first person they jacked off to. Me, with this image of them with an open *Teen Beat* magazine or *US Weekly* or the cover of *TV Guide* in front of them, there on the bed, on their navy-blue bedspread, the bed their mother made that morning, looking down at my photo in some magazine, and which one is it, and making a mess on it. That.

So, this guy says, "I used to have such a crush on you." I don't want to make him feel uncomfortable by asking why his crush on me does not still extend into today or by commenting on other men's masturbatory confessions to me.

I smile. Maybe an "Oh?" Nice, try to be nice.

"I bet you've heard that before," or, "You've probably heard that before," from him. Oh, I don't want to get into a conversation about this. Guy, c'mon. You're pushing it, you're pushing it such that I will have no choice but to let those two things before, about the masturbating and why your crushing faded, fly out of my mouth. Don't push it, don't try to make the conversation bigger.

I give another "Oh?" or something. Try to let it go.

It was fine. I felt bad. You feel bad. You can't really be yourself, can't really say the things you would naturally or organically say. Can't really engage. You don't want to hurt them. When they come up to you like this, vulnerable, nice. Genuine, but not knowing how to say what they want to say. You protect them. You don't get into it with them because you're trying to protect them. Don't pull me in there or we'll see you hurt.

That kind of thing gets weirder, though, you know. Writer, musician, and actress Moon Zappa told me that many times guys would want to be sexual with her in order to "merge" with her dad, musician Frank Zappa. Great. Duly noted. The kind of thing you want to know before you let them buy you a drink.

SPRAY

I'm flashing on another moment. I'm 21. Shooting a film on location in South Carolina. Oh . . . there's a few things about this film, this moment . . . OK, first things first. It's nighttime and we're out. Me and some of the crew, maybe one of the cast. We're out. We want to go into this nightclub. They check IDs. The guy gets to me, checks my ID. Hands it back and shakes his head.

"No."

No.

I'm not getting in. He thinks what, that it's fake? That it's not right? It's a California driver's license. I mean, prop departments on our sets used to make us all fake IDs back then, but hey, this one was real. I was 21. Was 21 and a half, or something.

"No."

I said, "What do you mean?"

"You're not 21."

"But, that's my ID. I'm 21, that's a California driver's license, what do you mean?"

"No."

What?

And then, here. Here. "You're Mallory. Mallory's not 21."

Christ. The character, CHARACTER of "Mallory" on *Family Ties,* the show I was currently on hiatus from to shoot this film, was a year younger than me. A FICTICIOUS YEAR YOUNGER THAN ME. So, I am not 21. I am not getting into the club. Boom.

Do I tell you about the rest of this? I hadn't planned on it. This experience, this time in South Carolina. There's really just one other incident, in two parts. No, I guess three incidents. Jesus. OK. We had rehearsals for this movie in LA before we flew to film it in South Carolina. OK, so rehearsals. I wanted it to look good. I wanted to rehearse as much as we could, take advantage of the time, you know? One of the other cast members was not into it and calls me a "Star Bitch." Now, OK. Why am I bringing this up, that's work-related shit. And, I really want to focus on Fame here and nothing else. You get it. But, this . . . OK, I'm talking about the film *Satisfaction* and I mention this because we were all in a band. All equals, good friends, but goddamn if my volume of Fame couldn't be looked past, at least by that one cast member. Shit. It took me by surprise. That sheath, that sheath of Fame that I'm looking out of and seeing everyone, all of us in the cast, as being at the same level, but the view outside of me, looking at me, was of the sheath. The Fame. So, I was "Star Bitch."

OK, we leave to go on location, to shoot the film. Now, I'm thinking I've got to get this off somehow, this sheath, to properly be in the band, right? Got to get this Fame off somehow. An average of 26 million people have been watching me, continued to watch me, on *Family Ties* every week, so the Fame is soaring, and right at, probably, its peak, and I'm thinking of ways I can shed it or obscure it so I can "be with the cast." First thing I do when we get to location, to South Carolina, is to get rid of my trailer, the motor home. That was the second incident. Production was thoroughly confused. My agent had negotiated that for me, everyone wanted that kind of thing, blah, blah, yeah. The rest of the cast had these small "honey wagon" rooms, so I thought I could just have one too. And so on. Tried to "be one of the guys." But I couldn't. It didn't work.

Third incident: There was a scene, shooting a big group scene for the film. I don't know how it started, but this same cast member blows up at me, more "Star Bitch," loud, and more, in front of the crew. Fuck. Cannot get it off. Cannot be part of the group. Will not be allowed. Fuck. You're just shut out. Not allowed. I don't blame that cast member. It was the Fame. It wasn't me. It was too much. Too much. You're different, you're up there, you won't be included.

Actor Treat Williams told me about this country store he would go into, near his house. There was this group he was part of there, ten guys, maybe. Drinking coffee, shooting the shit. He loved being part of this group, felt included, accepted, IN.

Then one day, one day, this guy in the group says, "Hey, Treat! You must have really needed some money lately, because I saw a film you were in last night . . ."

Treat's stomach tightened. He knew what was coming. You hope it's not coming, but you know it's coming.

". . . I saw a film you were in last night; what a piece of shit that was."

Fuck. You're Treat, imagine you're Treat. You love this place, this country store, the camaraderie, and with one sentence you've been excluded suddenly, cut out, set apart, far away. Treat unloaded on the guy. Of course. You would have done the same. And now he can't go back in there, not in the same way, ever again. That guy took it from him. He pointed at the Fame and took Treat's nice country store camaraderie away from him.

Fine. You're out. But there is this nice thing, this other thing. The flip side of that, where you are automatically IN when you're dealing with other famous people, people who have your level of Fame. The nod. "Wassup?" The Nod of Recognition.

"I see you. You, me. We get it. We get what's going on. I feel you."

It's nice. In an airport, at an event, across a room, "Wassup?"

OK, like I've said, Fame is this other "reality." It gets put on you. Some realities we think up for ourselves, but some are put on us. Other people are reflecting it onto you. You're not generating it. C'mon. Do you know how many people would be "famous" if you could actually self-generate this? Because, no, you can't. It gets put on you. Like every idea about you that someone has tried to spray onto you.

"You're not very bright."

"You're the prettiest girl in the world."

"You're excellent at cooking."

"You can't do math."

"You're amazing."

"You shouldn't be here."

"You don't have good ideas."

"You could have the run of this place if you wanted."

You, you, you, you. Telling you who you are and what you can and can't do. Shit, some of it is good. Some of it is good to absorb. When someone is spraying their "reality" all over you and it contains, "You can do it, because I believe in you . . ." Yeah, spray that reality all over me, all day. The rest of it can fuck you up.

So, Fame is an "imposed reality." Someone sprays it on you. You're not making it real; everyone around you is. Anyway, that's what it's like, from the inside.

"Everybody's so different, I haven't changed," as musician Joe Walsh's song goes.

You're not any different. You don't feel any different, don't feel like you've just broken through into some higher level of understanding about life or accessed some way to perform miracles at will. Whatever, you're the same. But not your reality, the one you count on, the one we take for granted will just be there for us—the sun comes up and you get ready for work and your coworkers treat you a certain way, you go to a game on the weekends, your good friends are Mike, Sharron, and so on. The country you live in, the language you speak, the gender you are (or want to be)—you've got a handle on your "reality." Fame interrupts that. It hijacks it. Fame hijacks reality. I had a reality about me and my life and then I had Fame sprayed all over me and I was suddenly in another reality.

There's this great sociological theory from Hugh Mehan and Houston Wood about how reality is created. "The five features of reality." That you pick a position and then spin everything around you, all your encounters, to support that position. That the position is pretty ironclad if everyone around you is constantly reflecting that same position back to you. I mean, you hardy have to spin anything in that case. So, there you are, Fame sprayed on you in the form of everyone reflecting it back at you. Like everyone but you got the memo that you're famous. And at some point you don't know what else to do but to

just go along with it. You can't escape it being reflected back at you all the time. You're just stuck in
this new, imposed "reality." So you go along.

SEESAW

There's this time. I'm 21. I'm in a sushi bar on Sunset Boulevard. "Sushi on Sunset." Really, that was the name. I'm sitting in a booth with my publicist, the formidable Nanci Ryder. Maybe some other people are there, I don't know. She had a copy of a tabloid. She shows me the "piece." The headline and the picture. The headline was, "Justine Bateman's Trial Marriage Collapses," and it says that I'm "in shock" because my boyfriend "dumped" me. Pack of lies. Here's the thing, if you ever want to control a situation, here's the thing: when you tell more than one lie at a time, the other person will be so consumed with "setting the record straight," with rectifying the multitude of lies, that the objective of dealing with the actual liar, himself, will be lost. So, the tabloid used that, that tactic.

Yes, we'd been together, but it was never a "trial marriage." (Christ, I was only 21.) Yes, we had broken up, but I broke up with *him*. Neither here nor there, but hey. And no, naturally, I wasn't in shock. What I was in shock from, though, was this fucking assumption, this gall to just print whatever they fucking felt like. I sat there, looking at this. Looking at this statement, this assessment they were putting in every goddamn grocery store in America, that said something that wasn't true. Something that categorized me, that painted me like this, like something I wasn't, feeling emotions I wasn't. Characterizing me as someone who had reacted the way I hadn't. I mean, yes, we were together, yes, we broke up, but not like that, not with those reactions, not in that way. That's not me. They were spraying. Spraying their "reality" over me. I wasn't different. I hadn't changed, but they were spraying something on me and now everyone was going to see that spray and not see me. They were not going to see what really happened, how I really felt about it all.

Shit. I sat there in that sushi bar booth and just felt fucked. Not only had the reality of Fame been imposed on me (there were some advantages, sure), but here, now, someone else was deciding the way in which everyone, millions of people, were supposed to look at me. I HAD NO SAY. So, this is on the cover of this tabloid. Inside, I open and look inside, and there's a big picture of me and my (now ex) boyfriend. My face has been altered in the photo. There's a picture of the two of us and the expression on my face has been changed by using what looks like a pencil eraser. It looks like the job that woman did on Jesus' face when she attempted to "restore" the Spanish fresco painting of him. Pre-Photoshop. Terrible. There I am with eraser-face, so I don't look like I'm smiling, so I have an expression on my face that fits the article, and I read the "quotes" that surround the eraser-face picture. Quotes, as if they actually interviewed us, or people we know. Just made up. Complete fiction. Just made up every quote they attributed to both of us. "Says a pal of the actress" and all that shit. Anyway, what are you going to do. But there, that moment, the first time a publication had pushed me out there as something I'm not, something I'd now see reflected in strangers' eyes on the street, something I had no fucking say in, no way to stop. So UTTERLY UNFAIR.

Yeah, I can hear it.

"That's what you get. That's what you signed up for. That's the price, the cost of being out there." See, these are the assumptions you get. Think of it. Maybe you've had something like this happen. Someone spreads a rumor about you. Something untrue or that twists the truth and it spreads like a virus and you can't get it back. Now everyone who heard it will look at that spray on you, and not see the real you. And you had nothing to do with that. They are imposing a reality on you that you had no say in. Maybe that drives it home. That's how it feels. But hey, I'm not here to pull you under the waves. This is me, in the water.

It kept going, the lies, over the years. Lies about my relationship with the cast and crew on the set, lies about my picking a fight with Madonna in a nightclub bathroom, lies about romantic relationships I'd never had. Lies, lies, lies. I'd live. I mean, here I am today, but it kept going. Hit after hit. Sometimes it was a hit from a publication, sometimes it was a hit from someone in the public, and sometimes from a family member. You'd get hit with stuff. Why are they hitting you? Did you do something to bring this on? Nah, you just have the Fame. You have the ball. No one is trying to tackle the players who don't have the ball. You touch the football and you are the target. Bring him down.

It's for a lot of reasons, why they do it, the hitting at you. Resentment, or fear that they won't reach their own goals, or that they don't measure up, or that they're more deserving of your Fame than you are. For some, the hitting completes a "perception of balance." What if every life is a seesaw. There I am, I'm famous, 21, making money like that. There I am, sitting at the top of my seesaw. The other side is down, resting in the dirt. I'm sitting high. Another person, the one hitting me, is on her own seesaw and she's on the end that sits on the ground, against the dirt, that's under a layer of sand. This person looks up at the raised, empty end of her seesaw, with the sky behind it, the upper end of her life, her as-yet-to-be-lived "highlight of her life," and she believes she will get there one day. That the end she is now sitting on, there in the dirt and the sand, will rise to that height someday. Rise up, and the other side will descend to the ground and rest on that thin layer of sand. OK, so that's the assumption, that "perception of balance." You see where I'm going? In order for that to be true, me, sitting at my height, I must descend. I must fall somehow, I must eventually come to rest in the sand or the whole thing is shit, this theory. Just a shitty lie someone fed this person to give her hope, to make her think that "things are going to be better." Just a shitty, shitty lie. If I stay up there, if I never descend, then I disprove the "theory" that these seesaws move, and that's a motherfucker.

"Oh God. What if it doesn't move. What if that is my lot in life. What if I am always down here? Always stay here. Always." Then, "NO. No, that can't be true." Knock those seesaws into motion. That's what the hits do. The lies, the gossip, the rumors, the hits. They knock the seesaws of the famous into motion, so that "perception of balance" theory can be true, Goddammit. Make it true.

DIFFICULT

I'm thinking about these two incidents, these two photo shoots. Damned-if-you-do, damned-if-you-don't situations. One shoot where I went-along-to-get-along and ate the results. And one where I pressed against it all, made an uncomfortable situation, but got dynamite results. OK, the first photo shoot. NYC, makeup on. Terrible. Conventional. Not who I am. Not me. Some idea of me. I hate it. I hate it. Been here before. Different people, who knows who, putting makeup on me. An NBC special years before that, at the beginning. I'm so young. Makeup on and it's big and it's orange, the foundation, on my face, like pantyhose stretched across my face, suffocating my skin. It's orange. One-shade-fits-all foundation for all the NBC stars? Hate it. Go to my dressing room. I'm so young . . . Can I do this? There are so many actors here, they won't notice, they probably won't be able to notice, there are too many actors here. Rub it off. Rub the orange off and look at it on the tissue. Brighter orange on the white tissue than on my face. So orange. Rub it off. Better. Take down the eyes. Better. Go out, go back out. Too many actors to notice.

Avoid the makeup artists, don't walk near and they won't notice.

So, I had been there, that feeling. Of someone spraying, applying, some reality on you, some personality they decided was YOU or that suited whatever they'd wanted to have on their network special or in their magazine. You. Who are you? It doesn't matter. It's not part of the equation. NOW KEEP THE PEACE. Hanging over you, always, always, cautionary tales of other actresses, in the past, who were "trouble," who were labeled as "difficult." You didn't want that. That was the worst one. The end. The label that was the end; couldn't get any worse. "Difficult." So, you say nothing. You're 20. You don't know shit. You don't know the truth, that everyone in power, or who you assume has power, is afraid of you. Afraid of the youth, assumes the Power of the Youth. You don't know that. You won't know that until you're older, too late to use that knowledge.

So, you sit there, at the photo shoot. Hate the makeup. Conventional, boring, beige, oatmeal, no edge. Oh God, the hair. The hair is turning into a 'do. Conventional, conservative. Spraying the reality of a senator's wife "look" on you. You are inside, you are inside, alive. Like a buried body, a person who's been buried alive in this spraying of someone else's idea of you on you, all over you. You are inside and you can't speak up. SAY SOMETHING. You're screaming at yourself to say something. Speak up.

Say something. Like those dreams where you can't scream for help. You open your mouth and the sound won't come. Or those psychological thrillers where someone's been given an injection of whatever so that they are alive, conscious, but paralyzed, unable to move at all, while totally conscious of every horror happening to them, watching it. Like that. Lame, right? I mean, I'm talking. I am talking to the makeup people. Shooting the shit, making conversation. I am talking. But no, I say nothing. I say nothing useful, nothing useful for me. I fold into the spraying, I fold into the reality they are making for me, the molding of what I seem to be, appear to be, I guess, to everyone else. I am a victim? They are "doing it to me"? No, I can't get off that easy. I AM THERE.

Now, the second one. The second photo shoot starts. Big magazine. Profile piece. I don't know the makeup and hair people. Easier if you've worked with them before. Sometimes you get that. That makes it better. But, I don't know them. We don't "connect." AND HERE WE GO AGAIN. On with the makeup, the spraying. Shit, shit, the same thing. The conventional, the "nice," make her look "nice." They don't know me, didn't try to, didn't even read any interviews beforehand or ask me what I'd like, with the makeup and hair. Shit. Going the same way as so many photo shoots and TV specials from before. I can't. I can't take the risk. Can I? To dive into the "difficult" area? OH, CHRIST. Every day, someone, everyone deciding who I am, because of the Fame. Projecting, categorizing, deciding my box. Everyone who comes up to me, even in interviews, someone else deciding how I'm going to come off. Deciding for me, HAVING THE LAST SAY, the final edit. Deciding that I said that "snippily." Deciding that my own quotes weren't "quite right" for the angle they'd already decided BEFORE they interviewed me. The angle they'd already decided that the article, the interview with me, was going to have.

OK. So much of this. So much of this, but there's this photo shoot with me there, me participating. I'm not buried alive. I'm not paralyzed, only watching the horror around me and unable to say anything, to stop it. I'm *not* unable to stop it. I JUST HAVE TO BE WILLING TO BE CALLED "DIFFICULT." I take the risk. The "risk." I mean, I dive in. I know this is not a risk that they will think I'm "difficult." No, I *know* they will think it. They will say it. They will spread it. They will say I am "difficult." They will. It's not a risk; I know. OK. AWKWARD. It's awkward, but I plow in. The hair's not working. I say it. They try something else. Not working. An impasse. Awkward. I get some water. I go to the sink, I have a spray bottle; I don't remember which. I have the water on my hands and then I cover my hair with it. My hair is wet. Wet. I wet all their work, erase it. The makeup. The makeup isn't bad. It can stay. THE FUCKING CLOTHES are terrible. Conventional, "nice," "Make her look nice."

Trying their best, sure. Not their fault, I guess. The awkwardness. I grab something, something I can just hold against myself. I will make do, I will make it look like I want it to look. It will look like ME.

Too far in now to return. Tense, the photo shoot is tense. I PRESSED AGAINST SOMEONE'S "GOOD IDEA," the idea they sold the magazine on. The magazine had this shoot scheduled, this assignment of me. Shoot Justine Bateman, nice profile next to the photo. And the photographer is picked, AN IDEA OF ME IS CHOSEN, or no. I don't know. They decide on a look, an angle, a setting, a theme. The clothes are picked like that, to support that. Or no. Maybe winging it. Maybe they don't know what to do, the photographer, the stylist, maybe they don't know what to do, so they must present this non-idea with firm confidence so that people, everyone, thinks they know what the fuck they're doing. They're not bad people. Maybe they shoot a starlet a week, a starlet a day. They're just doing their best. They're not bad people. But me. I made a tense photo shoot. Everyone, probably glad when it was over. I was on my own in there. I was on my own, not wanting to make it tense, awkward, but I couldn't be buried alive again, under their spraying of a reality I didn't recognize. But, the picture was great. Yeah, great. Great picture.

The stupid thing is that the first shoot I told you about was a magazine cover. The photo shoot where I didn't say anything and let a horrible picture be made was a *cover*. I had to look at that picture of me-not-saying-anything, of letting them spray their reality all over me, for a full month. Walking by, driving by the newsstand, in an airport, at the grocery store, at the manicurist, the doctor's office. For a month, had to look at that picture, that perfect treasure trail back to that shitty, shitty feeling of having people-pleased my way right through that photo shoot. That picture of me throwing myself under the bus so that I could avoid the risk of anyone calling me "difficult." Right under the bus. You can see it now. I still have it. It's here in the book. And the other picture too. The good one. The picture of me making a tense, awkward photo shoot, but a great picture. That's here too.

So many photo shoots. I find them online now, shoots I'd forgotten about. Shoots you were supposed to do because you were famous. Agreeing to settings and props and sitting on BMX bikes (I don't remember), posing with a miniature horse (SHOULD remember, but don't remember), in an antique convertible (DO remember that. Hated copying some '50s theme), blah, blah, blah. Too many. Not representational of me. Too many, no time to get a handle on the different ways you're being presented, misrepresented. You try to get ahold of it, try to influence it. It gets better. It gets better later, but in the beginning, it's flying out of control. You can't keep up, you don't have the spine to grab hold of an image, a clear image of yourself and insist on it. You're 16, 17, 18, 19, 20; you don't know shit. It's all happening too fast, too fast to do anything about. You're doing school, the show, then this Fame. Much too fast. Unmanageable. Can only lie down in the canoe and let the rapids pull you downstream. Just lie down so you don't get hurt in the violently fast, churning, vibrating water. And the rocks. Just lie down and let it all blow past.

CARPET

More about the inside of things. Red carpets. In the beginning, you're approaching one, you wore what you thought was "nice" (ha-ha). You're approaching one, your publicist or a "handler" at the event is smiling tightly at you with one arm extended, "inviting" you to move onto the red carpet to stand before the cameras. Maybe you want to, maybe you want to feel like you are that person whom everyone wants to take a picture of. Even if it is just their job, the photographers, to take pictures of everyone who walks by this way, no matter who they are. Or maybe you look for some other way around this, maybe you don't want to walk down there. You look for some way behind the backdrop; you crane you head around that event handler's outstretched, "inviting" arm to see a way around this. Eventually, though, you do step onto the carpet and you feel different. You tell yourself there's something special, magic, even, about being on this carpet. You start to have an "experience."

Now here's where your level of Fame gets measured, here on the red carpet. The reaction of the photographers, the measure of your popularity when in the presence of other famous people, the reaction

of the fans, all of it. You want to know the temperature of your Fame? This is the thermometer stuck
in the mouth of your Fame. This is it. Not that you
really want to take its temperature. Shit, you just like
the work, the work you do, the acting, the music,
whatever. But no choice now, you've stepped onto
the carpet; your thermometer is in. When you start,
when you're new, you don't know this, about the
thermometer; you're just having the "experience."
You step out and there's a sudden frenzy with the
photographers.

They yell at you. "JUSTINE! OVER HERE! CAN
YOU LOOK THIS WAY?! OVER HERE. STRAIGHT
AHEAD! RIGHT HERE! CAN YOU LOOK THIS WAY?
JUST ONE MORE, RIGHT HERE! CAN YOU LOOK
OVER YOUR SHOULDER? CAN YOU TAKE OFF
YOUR GLASSES? THIS WAY! THIS WAY! JUSTINE!
JUSTINE! OVER HERE!!!!!"

Any time you look at a picture of your favorite
celebrity at some event, marvel at the calm de-
meanor. Be amazed at the peaceful, slightly smiling
look on your favorite celebrity's face because while
they were standing there, placidly, a wall of people
were screaming at them, all caps, while the picture
was taken. That's control. That's focus. So, this wall
or mob of photographers surges to life and snaps
pictures, so many pictures, WAY more pictures
than they could ever use, than they could ever sell,
enough pictures of you to paper a room. All you know

is that you can't see, from the flashbulbs. So they are screaming at you and also you can't see. You can sort of see where you are going, but you have a collection of rectangular lights seared onto the view of your surroundings, burned onto your retinas. A whole array of bright rectangles, high, low, right, left, some brighter than others, some fading from the first photographers, some bright from the last ones. But hey, whoa, what was that? That experience on the red carpet, wow.

It builds to that. Maybe not the first time you're out there, on the carpet, but it builds to that, fast. I remember one of my first times through that gauntlet, on that carpet. Nice feeling, people paying attention to me. Just being 16 and having people, adults, pay attention to you, it makes you sit up. So, wow. Here, seeing, feeling that surge of photographers springing into action.

Snap, Snap, "OVER HERE!" and all that.

And then, then, I could hear them behind me, asking one another, "Who is that?" "Do you know who that is?" Yeah. Not like, "Jesus Christ! Who the hell was that girl? She was amazing! I have to know her name!" No, not like that. More like, "Is she famous? Should we know her name?" Or even, "Do you know her name? I have to tell my editor the names of each person in the pictures." That's all. So, felt deflating. You're invited there, the show has been on, you're being recognized in public, all that. But you don't care about the photographer's questions. It's just a little jarring, a little confusing. That Fame, it's not really part of your reality yet, not really. That's not until later.

So later, you do it, you walk the carpets. You do it, you do it. Carpet after carpet. You get used to the routine. You know how to move past them, how to say "Thank you" to them and then start to move before you hear the cameras' shutters slow down. Like taking the pot off the stove before the popcorn stops popping entirely, so everything doesn't burn. Get yourself off the stove before you and the photographers are stuck, standing there, looking at each other. You, wondering why they've stopped taking pictures, and them, wondering why you're still standing there. Dear God, you would never want to be in that situation. So, you learn to move off when the cameras' shutter sounds start to slow down even slightly, you get that pot off the stove. So, yeah, you get to a point, after you become famous, where the cameras surge with snapping shots whenever you come near. It sounds like a fat man fell onto bubble wrap. Snap, SNAP, SNap, Snap, snap, SNAP, snAP, snap, SNAP. Almost all at once. Sometimes people are moving around you, to the side of you; handlers, people whom the news outlets have asked to pull you over so they can get a "quick interview." They are coordinating, scrambling, running, then waiting patiently next to you. Waiting to extend that arm of invitation and guide you over to CNN or to whomever they've just promised an interview.

I'm thinking of these two times. I wasn't yet only doing the writing and the producing and the tech. I hadn't even started the directing. I was still acting, thinking that was still the way for me. I had jumped out of the business to run my clothing company, OK, but then I'd been back at acting, going to auditions, for a few years. I had been back in for a few years. I was at my brother's premiere. A film he was in, maybe *Hancock*. So, I'm there, the Fame is different, my Fame, it's less, far less. I made it that way, I guess, or is that just what we tell ourselves? You can't control it, like I said before, you can't control it. So, it's less. I had jumped out of the business and had had a clothing company, but I had jumped back into acting a few years later. I was back in, as much as I could be. But, it was different. I knew I wasn't on that "wave" anymore. That wave of favor where all the work just flows to you and the Fame is growing and out of control at times, all that. Here, I don't want to get into the work, into career, but it's woven together in places, the work and the Fame. I'm going to try to keep it separate.

So the Fame, my level of Fame, at that point in 2008. I had started the writing and producing and tech and I loved it, but here, the Fame on the red carpet was not connected to that. I step onto the carpet before I remember, realize and remember, the Fame thermometer. Too late to find a way around the carpet, to walk behind the backdrop, and I kind of want to walk it anyway, just to see. Hey, why not, just to see, maybe I'm wrong. Maybe I have more Fame than I'm assuming I do right now. OK, walk farther. Step out. Pictures taken, fine, nice. But, then I hear the surge. Behind me. Behind me, I hear the surge. My pictures are being taken, they know me, maybe, maybe three-quarters of the photographers know me, maybe not all, but they assume, they know that not just anyone would be allowed to walk on the red carpet. So, they assume they should take my picture, even the ones who don't know, they assume I'm someone. And the ones who know, take the pic- ture, they know. It's part of the event. But fuck. I hear that surge. The one, the one I told you about, where some beast comes alive, some beast made of a mob of photographers, all at once. Like the insects and worms in Ooga-Booga that live inside the burlap casing of his skin or a school of fish that swim and move together, giving the appearance of one large beast fish. That beast comes alive, with that surge, BEHIND me, see? Not for *me*, not in front of me. And if I had never, ever experienced Fame before, if I had never before experienced years of that beast coming alive *in front* of me, of hearing that surge of activity that would happen whenever I neared the photog- raphers, I would not have recognized it. I would not have known. That surge was happening, I could hear it. I had been fine there, I had been fine, in front of the cameras there, but then I heard it. And it was behind me.

Let's review. What happened? What do you think happened? Yes. Someone more famous than me— my temperature was being taken—someone more famous than me had stepped onto the red carpet. Someone more famous than me. My temperature had been taken. Now, what's happening in front of me? You remember that pot of popcorn? OH FUCK. The popping has slowed, I had not said "Thank you" and moved on before this could happen. It happened too quickly. SHIT. My popcorn is burning in the bottom of the pot. I have to move NOW, it's happening, it happened too fast. Fuck, I had no warning, I wasn't paying attention. Shit. The camera snaps have slowed in front of me, yes. The photographers in front of me are now snapping at me with only one eye. They're looking behind me with the other eye, or maybe the camera is snapping, their hand holding the camera in front of them, snapping, but not looking at me at all. Maybe their head, the whole head, is turned away from what the camera sees, both eyes instead seeing the more famous person approach. Photographers' eyes are down the red carpet to see when they can start snapping pictures of the person, the more famous person behind me, farther down on the red carpet. I quickly move past to the next portion of photographers, move away from the surge. But fuck, it's all fucked up now. I mean, fine, not fucked up, just uncomfortable. Uncomfortable, and now the entire line of, the entire wall of photographers, knows who just arrived. You are not that famous now, compared with what is about to come their way, down the carpet. You're just not that valuable now. God. Get down this line of photographers, down this carpet. Get to the end, get into the theater, get off that red river and into a seat and watch that film. And in your seat you feel ashamed, as if you were responsible for your level of Fame. As if you have any control over the rise and fall of your Fame. Any control over getting the Fame in the beginning or maintaining it at a certain level as it rises. What can you do? You're not responsible. But other people behave as if you are. Maybe you are. Maybe you fucked it up. Who knows.

Sociologist Erving Goffman would call this a "performance disruption." The red carpet can be the capital P, capital D, performance disruption. Remember his theory? That everything we do is "impression management." Performances to manage what people think of us. How we dress (the costume), what restaurant we want people to meet us at for lunch (the set), who we want around us when you see us (the supporting actors). A performance disruption is when all that is tossed into the fire and you are no longer in control of what people may think about you;

you are at the whim of the situation. And you may come out of the situation looking a lot worse than when you went in. A lot.

There's this other time, at an awards show. Around the same time, I guess. (Wait, I'm looking at the pictures online now. Three times—I went to this awards show three times. Why? Why did I do this three times?) For years, I would only go to an awards show if I was nominated. I never wanted to hear the dreaded, "Well, what are you doing here?" Said nicely or innocently, or can that ever be asked innocently, I don't know. Maybe it's just shitty. A bad, mean thing to say to people. But, if I only ever went to awards shows when I was nominated, then I wouldn't be subjected to that, to hearing that question. No chance of someone taking a pot shot at my level of Fame, if I'm nominated, right? But, I pushed against that here. I went UN-nominated. (Three times. What the fuck? Whatever.) I'm at the Independent Spirit Awards, this is around the same time, 2007, 2008, 2009. (Three years, three times, like I said.) OK. I'm there, on the red (blue) carpet, and this thing happens. I don't know which one of the years, maybe all of the years, I don't know. That thing happens that you never, ever want to have happen to you. There's the surge-behind-you thing. Sure, that's bad, but you can manage it if you catch on fast enough when it happens. This other thing, no. You just never want this to happen. This other thing is having your Fame temperature taken, but instead, you're a baby, and babies can't have their temperatures taken orally. Can't put that glass thermometer in their mouths. Have to put it in the butt. So, up the butt, and what if it breaks? Shards of glass, blood, poop. Yeah (if you're still here with me), that's what this thing I'm about to tell you is like.

OK. I'm there. After years of frenzied Fame, can't-go-out-without-people-losing-their-shit Fame, it's nice to have had it lessened, and to now be at the Spirit Awards and be surrounded by an entirely different, wholly-based-on-quality-of-work Fame. Nice. I like being there. "My people," if you will. That's what I'm telling myself. It's really the only level of Fame that makes sense to me. It's solid, it's wholly connected to the quality of the work. OK. There, feeling good. Pictures, sure. Pictures snapped. Some people asking for on-camera interviews, most of them not asking. It's OK. I expected that. It's OK. I'm not in any of the films nominated there, I'm not on a TV show, even. I'm writing, producing, digital media, the Future of Entertainment, and all that. It's OK. BUT THIS THING. OK. You don't want this. This . . . (Now look, don't get your hopes up. I'm not about to tell you that someone shanked me there on the red (blue) carpet) . . . I'm having some pictures taken. Still famous enough, I guess, for those pictures to be taken. Respect. OK. Then, this. This thing.

"Can you just . . ." The gesture. The look, with

behind the step-and-repeat backdrop, behind the red carpet, with Gia. Danny, not believing that escort actually fell for that, fell for that "Can I see the tickets real quick?" That he actually let Danny get his hands on the tickets. The escort, following Danny, running after him, into the theater practically, and yelling at him to come back and walk the carpet.

"That wasn't cool!" Yelling at him.

And Danny, to him, "Fuck you. That *was* cool. Fuck you, you don't hold these tickets over me." Fuck you.

People trying to touch me (1990)

On hand to celebrate Justine Bateman's 17th birthday were some of her best pals: Kari Michaelson (*Gimme A Break*), Justine's *Family Ties* co-star Michael J. Fox, her brother Jason (*Silver Spoons*) and *Facts of Life's* Mindy Cohn. Everyone had a blast!

Fake birthday party (1982)

Left: Solid Gold Howard Goldmann and Kelly Cutrone (with Baroness Sherry) (1990)
Right: Solid Gold Billy B. (1988)

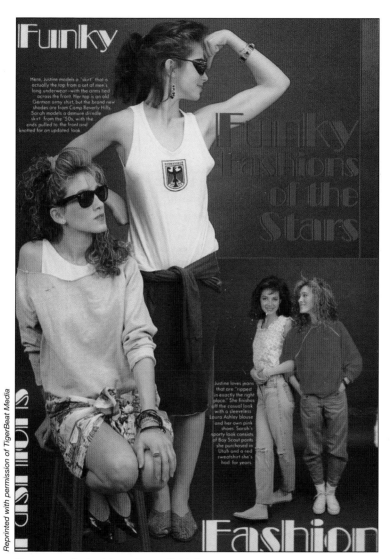

Garage sale fashion shoot (1984)

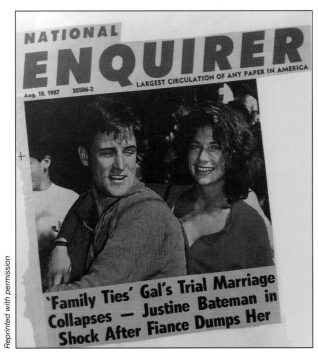

Sushi dinner reading material (1987)

Eraser Face (1987)

Elías García Martínez, *Ecce Homo* (1930)
and Cecilia Giménez restoration (2012)

"Star Bitch" (1988)

Me and Jason at our first red carpet event (1982)

Motocross bikes! (1982)

Miniature horses! (1982)

Faces & Places

JUSTINE BATEMAN

CURRENTLY APPEARING IN: *Family Ties*, on NBC

BORN: February 19th, 1966; Rye. N.Y.

LIVING IN: The Hollywood Hills

STEADY: Bobby, a production sound mixer

HOBBIES: Writing poetry, skiing, motor-cycle riding

SPECIAL GIFT: "I've got a wonderful eye for cops. I love to drive fast, but I've never gotten a speeding ticket."

The good photo shoot (1986)

REDBOOK

June $1.50

NEW!

JANE FONDA'S
EASY EXERCISES
FOR BEGINNERS
TRIM AND FIRM
HIPS, LEGS, FANNY

WHAT'S THE BEST CUT,
THE RIGHT CARE FOR YOUR HAIR?

DIETER'S CLIP-OUT
CATALOG OF TREATS
68 SNACKS & SWEETS
UNDER 100 CALORIES

FAMILY HITS!
LIGHT MEALS IN
20 MINUTES

BEAUTIFUL
SUMMER LOOKS
14 EVERYDAY BASICS

IS YOUR MARRIAGE TIRED?
HOW TO WAKE UP YOUR
LOVING FEELINGS

CHOLESTEROL ALERT...
DON'T LET BAD FATS
ATTACK YOUR HEART

● A VISIT TO VICTORIAN
SHOWPLACE HOMES

JUSTINE BATEMAN
GOES FROM
GIRLISH TO GORGEOUS
SEE HER GREAT LITTLE MAKEOVER
OPEN HERE ▶

That cover photo shoot (1986)

Publicity handlers (1987)

Jason & Justine
Bateman

The Gold Dress (1987)

1980s in Western fashion
Page issues

文A ☆ ✎

Among women large hair-dos and puffed-up styles typified the decade.[1] (*Justine Bateman, 1987*).

Mr. Blackwell, the people have spoken (1987)

Get out of the way (2009)

Hearing the surge behind me (2008)

UCLA Class of 2016

Where the paparazzi waits for the *SNL* hosts (2017)

Me on stage, wondering if I'll be shot (1989)

One of the highlights of my Fame (1985)

Shia LaBeouf's red carpet rebellion (2014)

A cautionary billboard in Hollywood (2014)

ISHMAEL

I tried to control Fame once. What a mistake. I was doing some press for *Men Behaving Badly*, this NBC TV series. 1996 or so. I had been through a lot of personal growth before getting that series, but no one knew that. That wasn't for public consumption. It didn't matter, for the interview. It should have been enough that I was just on this new TV show, right? "Here's Justine Bateman's triumphant return to series television"; something like that. So, there's this reporter, interviewing me. On the soundstage for the show, during rehearsals, up in the empty audience bleacher seats. We're sitting there, having our interview. It's fine, it's nice, talking about Rob and Ron, my character, normal stuff. Then he says this thing. I should have refused it, refused this fucking bait he dangled in front of my face. Near the end of the interview, the reporter puts his pad of paper and pen down in his lap and looks at me. He puts them down as if he's not sure he even wants to write this piece on me now. That's in my head only, maybe, but that's there.

Looks at me and says, "I don't want this to just be a puff piece."

I'm thinking, imagining, that he may not even submit this interview now UNLESS I "give him some-thing." Yeah. Probably not even true. He probably would have submitted the interview fine without me handing him "something." But me, wanting to "come back," wanting to ramp that Fame back up to the impossible-to-get *Family Ties* level, imagining that that was possible, that I had any control over that at all, I decide to throw my recent personal growth, my private personal growth, into the fire, under the bus, sacrifice it, in order to "attain greater Fame."

Yup, I fucking did it. Me. Surprised? I was. In the moment, I assured myself that it was worth it to "regain the Fame." I justified it by imagining all the "people it would help" to hear my personal, private, sacrificed information. Fuck. It was the only time I have ever tried to "regain Fame." It was an enor-mous mistake. The reporter was really happy. Maybe he'd tried that trick on 20 other famous people and I was the first one to fall for it. Me, the Fame veteran, the publicity expert. I fell for it. I was telling him all this stuff, really easy fodder for the public. Recov-ery, spiritual growth, all that. Fucking personal, not for public consumption, not for parsing in the public eye, not for picking apart like crows on a dead rac-coon in the middle of Main Street, while everyone stands around and stares. No. That information was not for that, but I dropped it there. I just threw it right there on the road.

* * *

You know the Bible story about Isaac and Ishmael? God tells Sarah and Abraham that they're going to have a kid. They wait, and no pregnancies for Sarah. Wait for years. Sarah gets old. Impossible for her to conceive now. Sarah then tells Abraham to go ahead and have sex with the slave girl, so they can have that kid God mentioned. So, Abraham does it. Has sex with the slave girl, and later out pops Ishmael. He's not the kid God was talking about. So, now Abraham and Sarah have two problems. They used to have just one problem, but now they have two. They still don't have the kid God was talking about AND now they have the Ishmael kid to deal with. Later, Sarah, at 90 years old (of course), gets pregnant with Isaac, the kid God was talking about. And Ishmael becomes a thorn in Isaac's side.

You get it. When I gave the reporter "something," I made "an Ishmael." The one time I ever tried to control Fame, I made an Ishmael. I first had just the one "problem" of thinking I didn't have enough Fame. After the interview, I had two problems: I still didn't have that level of Fame I thought I needed AND I had spit information out there that gave people some additional boxes to dismiss me into. Used to be one problem, now I had two problems. I tried to control something uncontrollable. And it became a thorn in my side. For years after that, whenever some other famous person was going through what sounded similar to what I had spewed about myself, I'd get an urgent call from a talk show or a news show, to "comment."

"So-an-so just did this-and-that. Can we get your comment? Can we have you in the studio to discuss this? Can we get your take on this? Can you come on Charlie Rose? Larry King?" No fucking way. I'd made an Ishmael; that didn't mean I was going to feed it. I was going to leave it outside, by the river, in the elements, like the Vikings did with their deformed babies. I was going to leave it out there to die.

VEIN

Shit, I think I'm going to have to start getting into the online troll attack stuff. This other time, I was on the TV show *Men Behaving Badly*, or I hadn't quite started that yet, I don't know. It was back then. I'm 30 or so, 1996, '97. I'm at an event. Pictures taken. Fine. Look online after. Just chat rooms, really, back then, but online. Hey, always a risky endeavor. Yeah. You are almost guaranteed to see something really bad, really awful, written about you. Some blog post, some comment, someone who doesn't know you, will never meet you, just cutting you open, stabbing, hoping in this stabbing into this body, in this black online room of not-knowing-you, hoping somehow, in the dark, to hit an artery. Or at least a vein. Hoping to make it bleed. One comment distilled down to a sharp enough point, on an accurate enough stab, that lands "right," really hits its mark. That kind of comment.

The time that must go into crafting some of these comments . . . "If I was Justine Bateman, not knowing her, sure, but if I was Justine Bateman, what could be said, what would hurt the most, if I was Justine Bateman?" And that's the one. Maybe someone just has a natural talent with that and it takes mere seconds to come up with a sharp enough and accurate enough dagger. Maybe for others it's more of a struggle, takes more preparation, more planning. More practice on other celebrities before they start getting a feel for how to get the sharpness, for how to have that accuracy, how to really get the blood to run. But they get it, eventually. They get into the rhythm. And then, it's easy. I mean, it just takes some practice and the vision of them as not-a-person, right?

"They're not-a-person; I've practiced my blade-making and my accuracy and I see results. I think I see results. I feel good. I feel better when I do that, when I cut and gut and make them (I think I make them) bleed." OK.

You cut and gut and make them bleed. Type, type, peck. Peck, peck, on the keyboard. Maybe you peck, maybe you can't type very fast, so you peck. Peck, peck, stab, stab, stab. The frenzy of it; that's energizing. "Maybe that's it; maybe I've hit the mark." Peck, peck, stab, stab. And then others are doing it too, and there's this sense of community, of friendship, of tribal ritual. Chum in the water now. Peck, peck, stab, stab, stab. The blood, the confusion on the celebrity's part. (Did you know that was going on? The confusion? The feeling of being gaslight? Maybe you didn't. There, I give that to you. I added you a vein.) Cut and gut. Hit a vein, an artery. Holy shit! An artery! HEY, GUYS! OVER HERE! I

HIT A MOTHERFUCKING ARTERY. LOOK! THEY'RE THRASHING ABOUT, THEY'RE FIGHTING BACK. HOLY SHIT! HA HA! WOW, LOOK! The celebrity is fighting back online, on Twitter, on reddit, anywhere. Others have joined in, dog-pile, gang-bang. Piling on and not stopping. Battling in the dark is you, there behind an egg, your profile-picture egg. Behind your egg and your one follower or 15 followers and your *Joined October 2013* profile information. You practice and you get good and you're performing! And fuck yeah, it feels good. Really stick it to those fucking celebrities.

"Those attractive, famous, rich fucks who look down on us and fucking get jobs so easily and I'm stuck here, hating myself, and YOU DID THAT, YOU FUCKING CELEBRITIES. I will stab you, I will eviscerate you with my new knife, the sharpened troll tool. I will stab you and find a vein in the dark with my online comments. My online comments, my tweets, my blog reviewing your movie that I thought was a piece of shit because I hate you because you are famous and rich and attractive and I hate myself and YOU did that. I fucking hate you. My knife is sharp and accurate and long. It is long and heat-seeking and I will not stop stabbing at you in the dark with my long heat-seeking knife of fucking comments and tweets until I find that soft belly, that Death Star weakness Luke found, that vein, that artery of blood. And I will watch that motherfucking blood run."

So, yeah. That's what it's like. So, here. At the premiere. I'm 30 or so, on a new series, or not quite on
it yet, and I'm bigger. You know—I'm bigger, heavier.
And I'm not thinking about this. Not thinking about
my size. I don't know. I'm not thinking about this while
I'm on the red carpet. I'm wearing this white cardi-
gan, soft, so soft. It's sort of shiny, you see where this
is going? Sure, I'm bigger, it's not that, the shininess
just makes it worse, makes it more pronounced; the
lights, the camera flashes bounce off, make me look
even bigger. Not an excuse, just an accent. Anyway. I
look it up online after the event. Comments about the
weight. Aw, shit. I forgot. I forgot that I was bigger,
bigger than the last time I was on a red carpet, last
time I had my Fame temperature taken. OK. Yeah,
you got me. Christ, everyone. The chum in the water.
Everyone "chatting" about it. Wow, really? But then,
in an anti–fat shaming moment-in-society luckiness,
a wave of defense rises up from others. And shit, I
don't want either. Don't want the comments about
the weight and also don't want the defense of the
weight. Don't want either. But you are the body, you
celebrity, the flesh for the knife, for the sharpened
and focused and practiced knife of online words. You
are the stuck pig and Fame is their target on you,
painted there on your back.

I remember bad times like that, years prior, but the
comments weren't so easy to manufacture, to get

out there, pre-Internet. If you weren't writing a fan letter, then you had to have the cooperation of a newspaper, a magazine. And these are publications that had a reputation to uphold, relationships to maintain, with publicists, studios, other celebrities. They had something to protect, to defend. The tabloids, not so much, see. Not so much. They were the early trolls. The in-print trolls. Still, there were times when both the "responsible publications" and the tabloids would get in a chum-frenzy, a blood-in-the-water hysteria, almost.

I got caught up in one of those. I didn't mind that much, I guess. The whole thing was kind of amusing. It was the Emmys, 1987. My second nomination. I had gone into the Mark Wong Nark store for a dress. It was on Beverly Boulevard, I think. Walked in and saw this gold dress. Designers didn't send you dresses for the awards shows yet. At least, I didn't know about it. Anyway, in the store, the dress is nice. Reminds me of an Emmy. The tight gold dress. Nice. With a little black bolero jacket. I'd do gold makeup, gold stockings, black shoes. Nice. No stylists, no one had stylists back then for awards shows. Me, 21 years old (you're getting a lot of 21-year-old shit right here, so far), just getting a dress I want to wear, to have fun in, look good in. That's it. I don't think about "how this will be seen." Not thinking about that, not at all. I go to the Emmys with my brother, we go. And pictures are taken. Fine. The usual. My Fame is at its highest, probably, so the surge, the cameras clicking, the frenzy, that's there. Used to it, nothing extraordinary. I don't win the Emmy. Fine. Rhea Perlman again. OK.

Now, next day. Next day, the papers, the tabloids, the "reputable magazines," fucking everybody is losing their minds over this dress. You can't be serious. Losing their shit over this dress. Lots of attacks, yes. Lot's of . . . Here, here are some of the quotes: *Too short, too tight. Skintight. A little outré. An ace bandage. A long girdle. Least amount of fabric covering a nominee.* Pretty tame, compared with today's comments, but the outfit landed me on the dreaded Mr. Blackwell's worst-dressed list. Sure, at first I was sad, disappointed. I felt attacked, targeted. But then I looked at the people on his "best-dressed" list and didn't like their style. People like the Queen Mother of England, etc. No offense, but that's not me. Now, on the worst-dressed list that year was actress/ director Diane Keaton, actress/director Lisa Bonet, and singer/actress Cher. This was company I was fine with keeping. So, see? No chum in the water there for me. Maybe I was just famous enough not to give a crap, or maybe I thought I looked good and no amount of "reputable publication" and/or tabloid pile-on was going to change my mind.

Shit, don't you fucking know it, as I'm looking up some quotes from Mr. Blackwell, something from that 1987 episode to give you, to amuse you, and I have to scan over another shitty comment about me that I hadn't seen before. Something about that 1987 worst-dressed list and me. *Doesn't act in watchable movies*. Oh Christ. OK. Getting you an extra Blackwell quote, anyway. Here: *A painfully stuffed sausage*. Was that worth it? Me getting scraped by that rusty metal edge of a shitty comment to fish out that sausage quote of Blackwell's?

ACID

I'll tell you about a time I really got ripped, wrecked, hit over the head by online comments, and couldn't shake it off. Had a hard time shaking it off, for a while. Look, it just happens. You're famous and people want to cut you. We talked about that. So, I'm doing a Google search of myself. STOOPID. Yes, I know. Quite dumb, you're right. Should never have dived in there. Stupid. Why? I guess you get curious. Want to know if you're still "in there"? Are people talking about you? Not the trolls; I'm talking about real people and reputable publications. You're taking the temperature. You're not on the red carpet, but you're taking a Fame temperature online. Looking. Stupid. (God, I want to get this date for you, of when this happened, and I hesitate. Don't want to put those search words in there, because I don't want to see that shit again. OK. Going to do it quick. Quick.) OK, about 2009. In 2009, I put my name into the Google search bar. *Justine Bateman* . . . and the auto-complete comes up.

The auto-complete says that the top option is, *Justine Bateman looks old.* I blinked. I wasn't even shocked. I was pre-shocked. I didn't have a container

for it. I was 43. That's it. Always looked young for my
age.

Justine Bateman looks old.

Did I? Really? I looked in the mirror. I thought I
looked OK. Looked fine. Hmm.

I CLICK. Yeah, that's right. I CLICK ON THAT
SEARCH LIKE A GODDAMN IDIOT. Right there. Oh,
I would love to have gone back in time and, right
there, grabbed my little index finger on my right hand
and pulled it off the fucking mouse. Pulled it off so I
could not click, so I could not let this disease into my
head that would stay there for years. So, I click. Like
an idiot. Like I'm Gretel and the witch uses candy
to get me into her gingerbread house with the oven,
only she doesn't even use candy; she's holding out
this moldy crust of gingerbread, maggots in the ic-
ing. I know what's in store for me. Is this delight-
ful? Is this interesting enough to me, to look at that
moldy gingerbread, that *Justine Bateman looks old*
piece of lure, and think I should click? Go into that
gingerbread house, because I want a big plate of
that? Jesus, I don't know. What made me do that?
Arrogance?

"Oh, there's no possible way someone really thinks
that. Based on what? What evidence are they talking
about?" This is me, not knowing "them," whoever
has said this thing. I don't know them. They don't
know me. But the Fame, yeah, the Fame. My years
and years of not being able to control what people

said about me and being so famous, but now not being very famous, relatively speaking. Not being so famous and still, STILL people are saying something about me, and goddammit, I must have *some* control now, now that the Fame is less, right? Some control over people saying things, even in this Mentos-in-a-gallon-of-Coke eruption rate of online comments and out-of-control celebrity attention on the Internet. I must have some control, because I'm not that famous now, right? Yeah. You tell yourself that, Bateman, and welcome to the House of Moldy Gingerbread Hell.

You can guess. I clicked and IT WAS SO MUCH WORSE THAN I THOUGHT IT WOULD BE. Yeah. That's right. I thought, knew, suspected, how can you not, that there'd be some moldy gingerbread. I mean, that's what the witch is holding out to me, to get me in there. Moldy gingerbread, so I have to assume there will be more of that there. Yum, what are you thinking, but OK. Well, instead, "Welcome to a bowl of sarin-laced acid soup, you idiot."

Justine Bateman looks old.

No, not just that. That's the moldy gingerbread I knew I'd have more of. This, the rest here, is the sarin. (Ooh, I can feel the acid in the soup trying to seep back in me as I look online to get some good quotes for you. I'll do it. I'll wade into that acid for our rowboat ride.)

Looks like the sea hag.

Did not age well.

Looked really old.

Looking rough.

Looks like she's 55.

Willing her to eat something.

Meth addict?

Awful, botched facelifts?

Poor health?

Has aged rather rapidly and had no body, either. She could have found work in an Iranian brothel, but now forget it.

Time has not been kind to her.

She's a smoker.

Why does she look so bad?

Looks like death warmed over.

Is she sick?

I've noticed she's aging poorly.

What the hell happened to her?

And my personal favorite: *Justine Bateman looks like Eric Stoltz in the film* Mask.

A couple of things. First of all, I feel poisoned now. I just stuck my hands and my arms and part of my body into that sarin-laced acid soup, to get some juicy quotes for us. Secondly, actor/director Eric Stoltz, in the film *Mask*, played a character with a rare disorder, nicknamed "lionitis" because of the disfigurement the face suffers as a result of cranial enlargements. You got that picture? He wore a full-face prosthetic. I mean, his entire face, besides his eyes, was covered with rubber. So, yeah. I look like that. Just like that.

And here's what fucked me up. (And, oh yeah, congratulations, you stabbers, you hit a main artery there. You did it. Good aim, thrust, carry-through, all of it. Very well done.) What fucked me up was that I couldn't get my head around it. Not at first. Going to sound arrogant for a minute here. It's not my intention, but here. I've always been pretty. Born with a pretty face. I never saw it as some accomplishment; just some card I got in my deck, like brown hair, two legs, etc. Just a card in the deck, a pretty face—or a face that this society thinks is pretty, more accurately. So, a pretty face. See, I had never been attacked for my face. I'd never been criticized for my looks. It would have been like a tall basketball player being criticized for being short. That would be bizarre. So, there I was. Sure, 43 years old. Sure, don't look 16. So what? Never wanted to look 16, even when I was 16.

I mean, that's the irony. (I made a video about this; you can watch it online.) I couldn't wait to look the way I finally looked at 43, or the way I look now at 52. Oh man, I couldn't wait. When I was younger, I would look at European actresses with cheekbones and dark circles under their eyes and lines on their faces and I would want that. I would look with envy. I wanted to look like that. I wanted my face to represent me, to reflect who I was. Moody and dark and mysterious and deep. Not pretty and wholesome and available and approachable and all-American. Now listen, I didn't think about this before I was famous. I was fine. Fine with the pretty face, whatever. It was fine. It was after, after I became famous, that I began to resent that my face, or how I imagined my face, was betraying me. That this nice, wholesome, BEIGE actress girl type that everybody was projecting onto me, this hope and desire that I was all that AND that I was also just like the character of "Mallory." Oh, that was the ultimate dream, I suppose, the idea that I was just like her. Living, breathing, walking around. Available. Well, not me. I love her, she's mine and mine in a way no one else can ever have, but no. Not me. She is not alive, doesn't walk around. She's dead in the TV. You can watch her animated by the magic of reruns in there. That's where she lives.

So, my opinion of what I looked like from 16–21 was one of slight disdain. Not a rejection of me, of my face, but that my face seemed to make it so damn easy for everyone to project some reality upon me that wasn't me, didn't fit me. A reality that was bound to collapse and elicit their disappointment when I didn't play the part behind it, when I didn't support this reality they wanted from me. Obviously, I couldn't do it. I fucking tried. You know I did. I tried to be nice and smiled when people made their assumptions. And it became too great and over and over, and it tumbled over me. I felt I couldn't get out. But it was OK. I had my friends, my people. I told you about them.

So, the "lionitis," the "drug-addict face" these people assumed of me. (Oh yeah, how the tables had turned.) I didn't know what to do with that. It was so bizarre to me, so outside the realm of criticism I'd heard in my life, that I didn't know how to handle this. I wish, wish I had been able to skip over it like I did with the gold-dress-Blackwell's-worst-dressed-list episode. Maybe I could skip over that then because I was more famous. I could laugh in the face of that because I had company. Other actresses on that list who I thought had great style. To be on that list was to be in that group. Fine. But this.

Hey, I wasn't out there, you know? Out, as an actor, seeking attention. Why was I being hit? I was doing the writing and the producing and the digital media. I wasn't out there in the public eye, really, and yet the attack, the fury, the anger was as if I was very famous, right at that moment. And I wasn't. And so, I tried (oh, fatal mistake), I tried to "understand where they were coming from." I can't tell you what a wrong turn that was for me. Stupid. Bad mistake. Should have dismissed them all as maniacs and moved on. But no. Their comments were so bizarre to me, so outside the realm of things I felt could be critiqued about me, that I had to start to try to see it "their way." Yes, terrible idea.

I looked at the photo they were referencing. I thought I seemed fine. Another criticism, of another, different picture. Hmm, I seemed good, fine. I looked at one of these pictures up against a picture of me when I was 16. The 16-year-old face, OK, no lines, but big, round face, no character face, whatever. Not that attractive to me, for my taste. I look at the picture of me that they hate. The one of me at 43. I like it. I think I look represented. I look like "real me." Back and forth between the two photos, trying to make sense of it. Trying to see what they see, what they have discovered about how I look. I do this over and over. (Yes, I know. Bad.) I do this, because I can't understand what they're saying. And so many people are saying it. So many people, whole message boards. So, what, I'm right and they're wrong? All those people are wrong and me, inside me, I'm right?

And here's where I make a decision that would partially wreck me for a few years. I decide that they are right. Christ. I just made myself cry. I just made myself cry hard with that line. Oh, that took my breath away. Didn't see that coming. See, I've "worked through all this." I've processed this. This, this episode was years ago. Years ago. You little sarin-laced acid-soup piece of shit. You really worked your way in there, didn't you? You really stabbed it with your steely knives, didn't you? Little metal shards of acid sarin. in. the. blood. Oh FUCK. It's not so bad, don't worry. I'll be OK. Just crying a little. I've been here before. It's good. Flushes the shards out. It's fucking OK. DON'T WORRY. IT'S NOT YOUR FAULT.

Listen, I take responsibility. I volunteered to go in there again for our emotional time travel. I guess I had to, needed to. I volunteered to go in there and get us some juicy quotes. OK. I couldn't avoid this route. So, here we are, you and I. You, who maybe wrote those lines, maybe stabbed me with your steely, heat-seeking, long-range Internet comment daggers. Maybe it was you. Maybe you're reading this book right now and are ashamed. No, maybe you feel satisfied that you wrecked my perception of my face in a way that I could have never expected. Maybe you feel a twinge—no, not a twinge, a thrill of victory.

"I got that fucking actress, fucking D-rate actress who I used to jack off to, but who now looks *not* like the girl I thought I could be with, the one I thought I could take advantage of. No, now she looks like a woman, an interesting someone, and she stole it. She stole something from me. She stole that touchstone. Yeah. She stole that touchstone to that part of me, that version almost, of younger me that I really liked. She was a treasure trail to that part of me. But, now she's stolen it. She shut it up, dead and in the TV and not even retrievable through those reruns, because I know they are reruns and they're not *Now*. I can't get to Me Then, Younger Me, Touchstone Me, because I'm Me Now and I hate Me Now. I AM MISERABLE."

But, that's probably not you, reading this book, sitting in the rowboat with me.

OK, here's what happened. And there were other comments, sure, *she looks great* and all that, but I wanted the fucking, goddamn TRUTH. Because, you know, I'm all about that. And if so many people were saying that I looked like a crack whore, then they must be right, with me being wrong. I decided that I didn't look right, that I *did* look terrible, like something gone wrong. I decided that and I walked around ashamed of my face. That decision riddled my entire body with the belief that to look upon me was to look upon Horror. That people were choking back the bile when they had to speak to me face to face. That I disgusted them. That they were brave souls to be talking to me and allowing such pleasant looks to remain on their face during the exchange.

I began to feel grateful to each person for not collapsing in a pool of exhausted vomit from looking into my face. I began to feel ashamed. Yes. Every time I walked out of the house. Every time I sat across from someone at a table, over dinner, coffee, anything, and had a conversation. Every time a waitress would ask if there was anything else she could get me, every time a cashier in a store would hand me back my credit card and bag my purchases and tell me to "have a nice day." I felt the gratitude.

"Thank God I got through another day without

someone fainting from looking at my face." Yeah, you laugh. (Or you're one of those fucks who wrote that about me, so you're saying to yourself, "Damn straight. You should have felt the gratitude." Whatever, I'm not talking to you right now.) Hell, I'm laughing too. How did I do that? Make that kind of decision?

I'm willing to break it open right here with you, right now. What would it have meant for me to reject that, that whole batch of comments, users, all those people saying those things? To decide they were wrong and I was right? What would that have meant? Well, let's look at the gold dress situation. I was able to reject that criticism. I wasn't alone. I was being criticized for my style, for this one outfit, first of all, *and* I was lumped together with a bunch of other famous women whose style I liked, so I was keeping good company. Hey, there's even an awesome comment in *HuffPo* about that gold dress that I found when I was rattling around in there, on the Internet just now:

Justine Bateman's 1987 look . . . saw her reject the floor-length dress code for pieces she could actually wear. Red carpet style doesn't have to be stuffy or old; it can take risks, provoke conversation, and make challenges — which is exactly what Bateman did. By pairing a nude mini dress with a contrasting cropped jacket, she brought street style to an award

*show that lacked it. (And still does, if we want
to get real, which we always do.)*

Thank you, writer Anne T. Donahue. You're boss.
Oh, and the picture of me in that dress has been the
identifying photo for the Wikipedia entry for "1980s
in Western Fashion" for years. A real honor. Just sorry
Mr. Blackwell isn't alive to see that.

So back to the tearing open of Why I Let the Gold
Dress Episode Go, But Not the Face Disaster. To
reject the gold dress criticism meant, bingo, that I
would still be in this company, still keeping company
with all the other rad women Blackwell had also put
down. Now, for me to have rejected the face criticism
. . . that meant—oh Christ, this is going to sound
bizarre—but to reject that face criticism would have
meant rejecting Fame. Now, stay here with me. If
my Fame is faded, don't have much compared with
what I used to have, and the mentions I'm getting are
mostly toxic, then I have to choose. Toxicity Fame
or no Fame. And, you guessed it, I chose the Toxicity Fame. Unconsciously. It was unconscious on my
part.

Look, it's like this. You might have some bad relationship in your life. A parent, a sibling, a friend,
maybe even your mate, boyfriend, girlfriend, husband, like that. You've got this one relationship and
it's bad. You fight, they get under your skin. Jesus,

you hate being around them, really. So, you have a choice. You know you do. You can simply not be with them. You can not know them. Leave them, not go home for the holidays, stop inviting them over for parties, you can stop. So ask yourself: Why haven't you? What's holding you back?

For most people, it's usually this: "Because at least I have *something* with them. IT'S BETTER THAN NOTHING." It's better than nothing. See that? That's what I did. Unconsciously. That's what I did. I grabbed hold of something toxic because it was better than the nothing I assumed I'd have if I rejected it. Sure, it sounds like, "Oh, Justine, you poor thing. You poor victim of Fame. You poor casualty of Hollywood. You poor thing." But, it's really OK. It's just one of those deep-set, unconscious choices caused by an irrational fear.

Once you expose that kind of fear, it begins to die.

TRAUMA

Let's unpack something else. *Why* did I want that, that toxic Fame? Why? I'm asking myself. This goes back to that reality thing I told you, when someone projects a reality on you, sprays it all over you. You get used to it. Especially Fame. Fame isn't some reality that exists in only one place or instance, like the way your parents treat you *only* when you're home for the holidays, back in your hometown. Fame is a reality that you cannot escape anywhere. Everyone is in on the plan. Everyone. Every friend, every cashier, every cop, every employer, every flight attendant, every shopper, every moviegoer, everyone. You press against "the reality of Fame" at first, sure, because it's so bizarre, but that becomes exhausting. You finally, after a while, you finally relax into it.

You say to yourself, "Hey, I didn't think this was real, maybe I still don't think it's real, but this is my reality." You sink into it. You stand on it, even. Feels pretty solid. You jump on it, up and down. It's solid. It's the glass walkway over the Grand Canyon. You know that? The Skywalk? The glass you can stand on and it's as if you're levitating over a 700-foot drop. That's how the "reality of Fame" feels when you first start really letting it in, letting it become a foundation in your life.

So, we all do it. And there I am with this floor to my life, this reality I'd known for almost twice as long as I hadn't known it. Pretty solidly, my reality. Even with it at a lesser degree, still a reality. So, when I saw those comments about my face, it was as if all the reality of Fame in my life, the totality of an enormous component of the reality of my lifetime, had been distilled down to this collection of face-bashing comments. Like I said, I wasn't on a show, wasn't pursuing Fame, even, just writing and producing, and in the digital space. So, the only Fame I saw reflected back to me that day was all the nastiness about something I couldn't myself see, didn't agree with, but goddamn if I didn't straight-up grab hold of that. Fame had been distorted in that moment into a grotesque fistful of moldy gingerbread acid soup and I took hold of it. Like the passing of a baton, I received the handful of mold and acid because, I guess, "it was better than nothing."

Now, look. I know, I get it. Someone's going to pull that one realization out and put it in an article or a blog post and they're going to title the entire piece something like, "Justine Bateman Was So Desperate to Hold Onto Fame Later in Life That She Was Willing to Believe Internet Trolls About the Condition of Her Face." That might happen. Hey, I expect that. But, that's the risk I'm willing to take for our emotional time travel. For you to see what it's like on the inside when you process Fame. At all the stages. The Beginning, the Love, the Hate, the Slide, the Descent, the Without.

I thought I would get to a pure "Without" stage in my life. I thought that someday the Fame would fade completely. When the Fame started to fade—not in the slow "Slide" stage, but in that fast, sand-through-your-fingers "Descent" kind of way—I thought it would eventually go completely. But really, it's more like a lobster trap. (I like analogies.) At first, Fame seems like something maybe you can go into and then come back out of later, but it's really not.

"You can check out any time you like, but you can never leave," from the Eagles' "Hotel California" classic. You will never be not-famous again. Society won't let you. The Internet won't let you. Everything you've ever done is there online, so immediately accessible that it's as if you *just now* did whatever is in that article, on that website. Hey, maybe that's why people get so upset when they see famous people get older.

"I JUST saw them! I saw them the other day online! They looked great. What the hell happened?!" They were looking at a 30-year-old picture online, that's what happened.

The truth is, I wasn't thinking about holding onto Fame at all when I saw those "face comments." I really wasn't. It was an unconscious gesture, to grab hold of that moldy gingerbread acid, to keep some of my reality. Do you get what I'm saying? We all have these sections of our realities. We are this kind of person, treated in this kind of way, with this husband or kids, living in this town, with this job, or this status in life, and these are just our realities. When any one of them, if any one of them were to suddenly disappear . . . God forbid your husband suddenly dies or you suddenly lose your job or have to suddenly move out of town or you suddenly live somewhere and you don't know the language or you suddenly lose all your money. Now, everything I just listed there is trauma-filled. Hugely traumatic. All of it. So, you can imagine what it's like when you have a large component of your life, your Fame, suddenly removed from you. It's not just that you can't get restaurant reservations as easily or quickly as you did before, or that you don't really have much Fame currency to inspire employment the way you once did (though that's an additional reality that gets pulled, but we're not talking about the work stuff here), or that you don't get invited to the parties like before. It's that an entire portion of what you came to understand as your life, your real life, your reality, has just disappeared.

And I'll tell you, when that happens, if you had anything in that safety deposit box before they blew up that bank that is your life, you're pretty well fucked. You gotta get it all out. Before it blows, when you first hear of the plans to set off a bomb. See, I'm talking about when you feel the Fame start to slip. When it starts to descend. You can salvage some things, you can grab some things before it's too late. You know what's in that safety deposit box. Your self-esteem, your ego, your self-identity, your self-perception, your understanding of where you fit in this world, your self-respect, your self-worth, your understanding of what your face looks like. You'd better get that all out of there before the bank blows, before your Fame gets yanked from you. Because if you don't, if you think for a minute that you're going to ride this out, that the bomb will never go off and that "those guys couldn't blow up a fucking chicken coop, let alone a bank . . ." If you think they can't carry it off, think that your Fame can't slip away, you are going to be sorry. You will be wrong, because the bank bomb is almost always successful. If you don't get it out, it will hurt like hell and no one will be there to help you heal. You will be on your own because no one will know what you're talking about when you mention your loss of Fame, of that reality. Your Fame will almost always fade, change, morph, whatever you want to call it, so GET YOUR SHIT OUT OF THERE BEFORE IT BLOWS. That's all I have to say about that. Get your shit out.

INADEQUACY

Sharing that stuff with you kind of fucked me up. Sticking my hands back in there, doing this emotional time travel with you. Looking at those situations again, reading those comments again. Hey, I should be past that, right? What's my problem. Why am I writing this fucking book? I should just stop now. Just trash it. Fuck it. Throw it out and just get back to my REAL life where I've forgotten about all those awkward, uncomfortable, confusing events that were generated in the backside of Fame. See? I don't feel this way still. Post-Fame. God, that's the meat of it.

Why am I writing this fucking book? Look, I didn't plan to come here to rip myself open and show you all. That wasn't my first plan. To make a bunch of gaping wounds and lay myself on a metal table and let you and your cadaver classmates poke around, tour my hills and valleys, my outside and insides, stick your metal tools in my wounds and marvel at the layers of emotional diversity, like sediment layers in the rocks lining the Colorado River. I planned to COME HERE TO TELL YOU a thing or two. Yeah, that was the plan. I'd gathered some really great, insightful, genius even, information, fucking wisdom, about FAME.

Who better to tell you than me, someone who has lived the whole life cycle of Fame and is fully aware of it, fully aware and able to analyze myself throughout the process. Goddamn special. All these theories. My Chutes and Ladders Theory, my "perception of balance" Seesaw Theory. Other theories, the theories from sociologists. "The Five Features of Reality." Oh, I had a whole plan to just expose you to that, I had pages and pages written, explaining that. "Mimetic desire." Had a few pages written explaining that. Thanks to Mary-Louise Parker for that one. Fuck, I had a whole book, you know, of just that stuff. A real arms-length dissertation. I was halfway through. I'd written half a book already that was academic and explained all these sociological theories. Half a book already. Not this emotional river. This wasn't the plan.

But, I'm here now, in this raw version instead. Here with you in the bottom of this well, where the river pulled our rowboat. Just talking about my shit. Fuck. This is not what I wanted to do. I should just throw this out. Just stop. But, why was I writing this book? I volunteered, stepped down into this black square hole, into feeling this way I felt years ago, to show you. I don't feel this way now. I think I told you. I'm happy with my life. I'm doing things I've always wanted to do, I'm the type of person I've always wanted to be. I have a great family and friends. I live with privilege. My most treasured possession is my privileged mind. Privileged, meaning free of the fear that used to live there. OK. I'm totally happy. So, what's the big fucking deal? Why did sticking my hands and arms and part of my body into the acid soup before, to get good quotes for us, fuck me up? Here. It took me into that dark section. It was all those quotes, a treasure trail right into that dark section of feelings, that black square hole of FUCKING INADEQUACY.

Look, here's the worst thing that Fame does to you. You have it, it's great. Nothing like it, but when it slips and descends out of your life, to whatever degree, you are viciously, I mean tear-at-your-flesh attacked, with inadequacy. See, N O T H I N G you do after you've been that famous is E V E R going to be good, or right, or applause-worthy, or impressive, or even fucking noteworthy. Your obituary will STILL, no matter what you've done after that great "achievement" of Fame, will still just list that pinnacle of "accomplishment," to the exclusion of almost everything else you have ever done in your life. And right there, you see, nobody wants to know about anything else, unless it meets that high level of attention. And with that kind of perspective, of course, the attitude is that you are an utter and dismal failure because you never attained that particular level of Fame again. That's ridiculous. I mean, here we are, rational people, and we agree that that's ridiculous. "Whatever happened to . . ." and all that. Ridiculous.

I can hear them, "Oh, boo-hoo. You reached the heights of Fame and fortune and now you feel bad, you feel attacked, victimized, even. Is that it? You poor little rich baby." OK. Yeah, yeah. First of all, just because someone's name is known, it doesn't at all mean they're rolling in cash. That's a fantasy. It's not reality.

Moon Zappa told me about the time she made an enormous effort to get as far away as possible from Fame and the machine that supports it. The temperature-taking, the accusation of inadequacy. She joined a cult. She had to join a cult to get away from Fame. She wanted to think about bigger things: mortality, human existence, things like that. But, she couldn't get away from it. The guru, the guru of the cult she joined, the cult she was in for six years or so, the guru had a Fame-based hierarchy too. The more famous you were, the better seat you got at the guru's appearances. I mean, c'mon. What the fuck. Supposed to be about spiritual enlightenment, soul-searching here. All Moon wanted was some kind of pure, real experience, and there in front of her were people more famous being seated closer to the guru. There she was getting her Fame temperature taken every time. Shit. Cannot get away from it.

What if you're married to it, to the Fame? You're not even being asked to measure up to some "pinnacle of experience" in your *own* life. You're being asked to live up to the pinnacle of human experience in your spouse's live. You've already got your own successes, your own professional successes, but people are pitying you, coming up to you and pitying you, always suggesting some inadequacy.

One wife of a famous performer told me it's as if people are always saying, "Your husband's doing so great. So, what are *you* planning to do?" This woman, with her own professional and personal successes, being pitied. "We just really want to see *you* do well, honey. We know *he's* doing great, but what about you?"

This inadequacy is this insinuation that the further you get from that "pinnacle of acclaim," that apex of Fame, the further you get from being perceived as a "success." A success. As if success is Fame and nothing else. Society has placed Fame on the high shelf. The summit of human existence. The ultimate achievement.

"Oh, you're famous, so you must have money, family, friends, invitations, career, accolades, everyone loves you, gives you things. It must be true." Fame. It would be nice if there were an all-inclusive package like that. One "achievement" bundled together with all that.

And you've heard it before, from famous people, "It's not all that. It's not what you think." But, we don't want to believe that. No. We don't want that to be true, that it's "not all that." We want to believe that there is a lottery ticket, an everything-could-change-in-this-instant-and-all-my-dreams-will-come-true kind of lottery ticket out there. Maybe it makes someone's today go better, faster, believing that everything could change in a snap and they could be famous and get that "whole bundle": the friends, the family, the love, the money, the career, the opportunities, the parties, the limousines, the champagne-being-carelessly-wastefully-who-gives-a-shit-poured-over-your-head. The free-wheelin', free and easy and excitedly WOW. That lottery ticket, that chance. That "big break." That cure-all. It's like that HAS to be true in order to get through the day.

Sure, some of it's true, that "bundle of stuff." You do get a version of that bundle with the Fame, but in pieces, in chunks, not all the time, in hunks. And then not. Then it's pulled away, and all that. Yes, sure. That's why we hold that Chutes and Ladders structure, so we can have the possibility for even a perforated version of Fame and what we think it will bring us. Even a perforated version.

The trouble is the *extent* to which we have built a support for Fame and have therefore held Fame as THE GREATEST—we've put it up there—THE GREATEST ACHIEVEMENT A HUMAN BEING CAN EVER ATTAIN. So, you're famous. Wasn't looking for it, had it poured on, sprayed on. And then it slides, starts to descend, and you are seen as trash, as an irresponsible person, a waste.

"You ungrateful little mole. You let it go?! What the fuck is wrong with you? Why did you let it go? You HAD it! You hit the square and climbed the ladder. Holy shit, right to the motherfuckin' top! You had it and you trashed it. You ridiculous waste of time, effort, attention. We bought into you! We invested in you, watched you, purchased the same clothes, watched your interviews, looked at your photos. And you squandered it. You wasted it. Why didn't you water it? Keep it up? A little maintenance, is that so hard? Too much? Fuck, you had it right there in your hand. Oh God. You blew it. We are disgusted. We have nothing but disdain for you."

So, yes. "What are you working on?" from every stranger.

"What are you working on?"

And later, "Are you still acting?"

Pitying.

"I saw that you squandered your Fame, didn't keep it up, didn't maintain it. And my neighbors turned their backs on you, but not me. I'm here and I feel so sad for you." So pitying. "But, I'm here for you, so let me know, are you still even acting?"

Now hold on. While these things are being asked, OK, early on, when the slipping just starts, you're acting, sure, you're auditioning, doing that part of the work/career, but you are not currently on a film or a show. Hell, if you were, chances are you wouldn't even be in town. If the actor's in town, at home, they're not on-location-working-on-a-movie. OK. And you feel this accusation of inactivity with that question, because you have so little control over what people think of you when you're famous, of what all these strangers, who think they know you, think of you. You immediately know they will walk away from you after, not thinking about the cool show or movie you did last year or the year before, but questioning if you have squandered this Fame they bestowed on you.

This disappointment and pity isn't true everywhere. Writer/director Peter Bogdanovich told me that in Europe you are as famous as the best thing you ever did, forever. No disgust that you're not thrilling them the same way year after year. You reach it, you stay there. But, we're in America, so let's get back to it. Some people are approaching you, coming up to you because you are famous, still. They feel an ownership, even, of the Fame. They are checking in to discover its health. And they are not liking what they hear. They will walk away with a seed of disdain that will grow if you don't get your shit together and pick up the pace on the work front, or get in a relationship with another famous person, or have a scandal or something. And shit, maybe you're working on other parts of your life right now. Maybe you're building a family, embarking on personal growth, starting a vineyard, learning about World War II. All valid, wonderful, even necessary things. Accomplishments, even . . . No. They are not. Not if you had once touched that glowing, ephemeral pinnacle of human existence, that Fame. And, oh sweet Jesus, you actually held it in your hand, cradled it, ingested it, walked around with it inside of you, letting it emanate from your body, sparkle and pulse, for all to see. No. If you once had that, then everything else you ever do will be shit, compared.

"Call us when you've done something on par with that, with that thing that caused us to spray you with Fame. Call us when you've done something that gets all our attention like that again."

All the while, there is this baffling assumption that you, the famous one, has control over the Fame. You have none. Not by any measure, whatsoever. You don't. You had no choice about it being sprayed upon you initially and you had no choice regarding its intensity or its duration. You also had no say in the matter when it began slipping, and you have no control over it when it is sliding down the hill. You get no say. But, the public thinks you do. They think you are its master. And you are not. You are a rodeo cowboy strapped onto a bucking bull, your gloved hand (if you had time to get a glove on) shoved under the bridle, bound with strips of dark, worn leather. You are riding it, trying to ride it. You are not the master of Fame.

Picture a friend winning something at a neighborhood fair. Maybe your state fair. Someone you know, they win. Hey! They stepped right into it. The brass ring! Wow, what a great thing! Totally random. Their name was pulled out of a fishbowl. Totally random. Could have happened to anyone. But you, looking at your friend, you think there's something special about him now. Something, maybe you feel this unconsciously, something about your friend, you now imagine, something about your friend must have drawn him to be picked out of the fishbowl. Something. He's special. Now. Your friend. Special. Hey, you too, by association! The town knows now. Next time, you see a next time, that your friend has his name in a fishbowl, a raffle box, a straw hat. Next time your friend's name is on a piece of paper and in the mix, you expect him to get picked. Some part of you expects it. "Here we go again!" You nudge your neighbor, the woman standing next to you, with a roll of the eyes and a sideways smile on your face. You, sort-of-famous because you know the-guy-who-won-the-big-prize-at-the-state-fair. You smile and mock-roll your eyes at the absurdity of this sure thing, now. This winning result that is bound to happen to your friend again, because it happened to him before, he won before. There must be something magical about him. "He draws these things to him. I know."

You stand there with your half-smile, arms crossed in front of yourself. Rock back on your heels, maybe. You wait in calm excitement, muted excitement, because your guy, your friend, he draws these things to himself and you, famous-by-association.

But, he is not picked. They do not pick him. They pick that woman on the other side of the room. That woman with the curly hair and the blue sweater, the one over there who works at the grocery store. They picked her.

Your friend now, "Hey, can't win them all." He's fine with it. You don't have an emotion yet.

"Yeah, you said it." You clap him on the back. You two start to walk out.

"Better luck next time," he says.

You there, still feeling around for the right emotion, not yet finding it. Your friend is fine. He doesn't care. He knew that the first win was a fluke, like every win, like that. Random. Right piece of paper in the right part of the fishbowl, at the right angle for the right two fingers of the right State Fair Queen to touch, and not just slip past on her way to another folded piece of paper with someone else's name written on it. No, it ALL had to be right. And now it's not. Now it just isn't. Your friend is fine. YOU ARE NOT.

Later, you find the emotion. You are angry. A little angry. A little disappointed. A bit angry and dis-appointed and, frankly, a little disgusted. You think, maybe not consciously yet, but under the riverbed, you think that your friend really wasn't trying hard enough. You, somewhat-famous-by-association. Your friend, that sonovabitch, really didn't try hard enough to draw the win to him again, like he did the first time.

"He fucking . . . He betrayed me. My trust. Is that what I get? For being there? To be embar-rassed like that, in front of all those people. Me, somewhat-famous-by-association, rocking back on my heels, almost? Sonovabitch."

"Better luck next time." Your friend betrayed you, not a winner, made you look foolish, not a winner. Better cut that shit away from yourself next time. Cut that guy off.

We think this scenario is ridiculous. We would never do that. Sure, maybe not, but some people will feel that way toward the famous. Some will feel it with every famous person who is now a not-so-famous-person-anymore.

"Why do they look like that now? Why don't we see them anymore? Why haven't they been in a hit show since then? What happened to them? What have they been up to? Where did they go? Are they still alive?" Not even a Google search before asking.

OK, look. You've got me in that well, I'm there with you. We're together. You've got me in that black well right now, of those years, years ago, where this was raw and open and confusing. "Me Now," though? They don't want to Google it? What I've been up to? The life I've been living, here, out in the open? They don't know? Maybe they do. I should really draw you a chart. Maybe I will put one in here, for you, before I'm done. The Fame so high, it reached the sky. *Family Ties*, about 26 million people a week watching us, watching me. Everywhere you go, everyone stops, grabs you even sometimes. Hated that. The touching, the holding of the arm, the stroking of the hair, even. Fuck. Always hated that. So, Fame sky-high. No matter how bad it got, though, I always knew Michael Fox had it worse. It's true. Fame sky-high. Then me after the show, theater plays, pilot's license, indie films, scuba certification, self-discovery, performance art, trapeze training, clothing company, acting again (it's all in the bio), writing, producing, digital media, UCLA freshman, graduating, writing this book, writing/directing/producing film projects. OK, you're caught up. That's me. What have I been up to? That's me.

"The chart will show, ladies and gentlemen, the chart will show a direct inverse correlation between her level of Fame and the degree to which she was/is an interesting person."

This is funny. You have these two lines. One showing the level of Fame you have and the other showing the degree to which you are an interesting person. For me. Maybe other famous people were more interesting when they were famous and not so much now, I don't know. For me, I became far more interesting as the Fame receded. I don't think there's causation there. Fame didn't make me less interesting, nor did I become more interesting because the Fame faded. The point I'm making is that while some in the public are watching the Fame trajectory, the line in descent, they are projecting upon me that my entire life is in descent. You see that? They then feel on solid ground, when they, not googling me, not imagining a life that could be happy or satisfying or interesting outside of Fame, away from that pinnacle of human existence, when they ask with a tinge of pity and a tiny edge of angry disappointment, "What happened to her?" They are looking at that line.

They are imagining, "Dear God, what if I had been at that level, had ingested, gobbled, that glowing ember of the highest success of Fame and seen its sparkle, its emanation, reflected back to me in the big, fully dilated, dewy eyes of everyone with whom I came in contact. If I had had that with its bundle of all the good stuff, you know, the money, the everything? And then if I was walking around now, like this, away from that pinnacle . . . Well, I would just want to die."

Oh, I'm bringing you back around. The inadequacy. Remember? Why would all this talk remind me of that black square pit, from years ago, of the feeling of inadequacy? Because no poetry writing/reciting; or play performance, off-Broadway or Berkeley Repertory Theatre or Williamstown Theatre; or private pilot's license; or indie film with great people; or performance art productions; or one-of-a-kind hand-knit and ready-to-wear clothing company; or digital media production creation; or college-attending at 46 for computer science; or book writing; or filmmaking is ever going to hit that Fame mark again. Honestly, I don't think so. It just won't. I won't ever be that famous again. And wanting, striving to hit that mark again is like trying to prove to some hard-to-please parents that you are still as worthy of affection as you were when they seemed to love you the most, when you were a four-year-old towhead. Ain't going to happen. Not ever. The number of elements that must be aligned for that kind of Fame to happen are remarkable. The right look, the right acting, the right project, the right company, the right network, the right night, the right time, the right era, the right moment in pop culture history, the right tolerance of the performer for that kind of attention—so many things have to coalesce for that kind of Fame to happen. Just bring down your expectations for anyone who's ever been there. It's not going to happen for them again.

OK. You win. Yes. Let's talk about actor John Travolta. The "Fame Unicorn." Sure. There's that exception. You're right. From TV's *Welcome Back, Kotter* and that Fame, to *Carrie* and *Saturday Night Fever* and *Grease* (bizarre and unusual at that time to make a transition from TV to film, by the way), to a fall of Fame that landed at the foot of the hill with *Look Who's Talking Now,* to the resurrection of Fame with the film *Pulp Fiction* and then living up there, riding out that plane of Fame now. Highly unusual. Hardly anyone sees that height of Fame and rolls all the way down the hill and then sees that height again. So, yes. There is at least one unicorn. The rest of us either see it once and don't see that height again or we stay there for a lifetime, which is also unusual. Actors Tom Cruise, Brad Pitt. There are a few. Lifelong, sustained Fame. Small ebbs and flows within that too, sure, but up on a certain plane for a lifetime.

I mentioned that strange thing the other day to a friend of mine, another person also made famous by a huge hit TV show. I mentioned that strange thing where people want you to hit that point again that causes that same level of Fame to return. That nothing you ever do seems to ever satisfy that request. He reminded me that it's true for a lot of people. Not just me. For actor Henry Winkler and the cast of *Happy Days*, it was that. For actors Lisa Kudrow and Matt LeBlanc, et al., it was *Friends*. For the cast of *Star Wars*, it was that film, etc. That moment, that perfect combination of the right studio and release date, or the right network and night, the right cast and writing and moment in society where you captured something they needed, something they needed to grab hold of, and you reach a level of Fame and then you're long held to that standard. Unless something satisfies that "Fame quota," unless another project elicits that level of Fame again, many are going to hold you to that standard. No matter what, your "biggest success" will have a mention in your obituary, unless you do something of that level again to knock it off the eulogy list.

And so, there's this crushing disappointment that can set itself up in other people and reflect back at you. It then tries to set itself up in you, yourself. And you have to fight it. You have to list all these things you've done, to yourself, and you have to remember that any one of those things would look fine, would look tall, if it was not being held up to this moonwalk, this almost-impossible-to-attain level of Fame you once had. You have to ignore that there will be people who will be amazed that you're happy and fine without it. It's a constant feeling of not being seen for who you are. But, you're used to that, right? When you were very famous, a reality was projected on you of who you were. When Fame fades, the projection morphs and a different, even more presumptuous projection of reality is sprayed onto you.

Oddly, there seems to be an acceptance of a woman, post-Fame, if she falls into certain categories. If she is outside of these categories, the public reacts with confusion, disappointment, and that little edge of anger. The categories are these:

1. The Mom/Housewife. It seems acceptable if a famous woman on the other side of their "peak" becomes a housewife, if she appears to be someone who "gave up her career to tend to her husband and children." Maybe she occasionally appears in *Good Housekeeping* magazine when she promotes her cookbook. Feels fine, acceptable.

2. The Polished One. The public is also accepting of a formerly famous woman becoming the wife of a famous or powerful agent/executive/businessman/politician and appears to be consumed with maintaining a highly coiffed look. As some people imagine that her time is committed to hosting charity events and enjoying day spas, they assume that the woman is bitter and resentful that she had to give up whatever career she'd had previously and that she now has no career or vocation at all. Some people get very angry, incidentally, when a woman they assume is playing this particular part actually *does* get a job, post-marriage. There's a lot of, "She doesn't need to work, her husband has money!" or, "She got that job because of her husband!" Stay unemployed and the public will "get what you're about."

3. The Junkie/Whore. Another "acceptable role" seems to be that of an alcoholic or drug addict. Recovering or active, it doesn't matter. The public appears to be "very understanding" or at least thrilled that a woman who used to reign from the top of the Fame mountain is now, they assume, stumbling

about in the muddy puddles in the darkness of the valley. It really justifies the Seesaw Theory.

4. The "24-Year-Old." Certain people also very much enjoy a formerly famous woman whom they assume just can't get past "the loss of her youth" and appears to be desperately trying to recapture it by dressing younger, etc. They really seem to relate to that, somehow. The public is pretty passionate about this option. A woman in this role will receive the most vigorous reactions. There will be a lot of criticism of what the woman is wearing ("Why can't she dress her age?"), how she styles her hair ("What is she trying to prove?"), and the age of whomever she's dating ("He's WAY too young for her"). They are drawn to a desperation they assume of the woman and they then set to attacking everything they once worshipped as her assets. She is accepted and "understood," regardless of the toxicity of that acceptance.

5. The Plastic Surgery Slave. Her aging face, especially, will be ripped apart (figuratively) until the woman rips her own face apart (literally) with plastic surgery. Maybe it's "for herself" or maybe it's to quiet the cacophony of criticism, but either way, it happens. There's a welcome party when she emerges from the post-op self-exile, when the swelling has dissipated. Some in this welcome party will applaud her, will say she looks great, but the some of the same critics of her aging face pre-surgery will now

express disgust and disdain for her post-surgery face. They will talk about her face endlessly. They will create websites exclusively dedicated to examining what they think she has and has not done. They will post photos of her with a smattering of red arrows and circles over parts of her body that they're sure she's surgically altered. They will not stop the speculation. But they are strangely accepting of this post-Fame role. They are critical, but not confused. They "understand."

All these "acceptable roles," these roles that people assume you will fall into, exclude the involvement in professional work, post-Fame. Pursuing another career seems to confuse the public. Seems to make some people angry. Maybe it upsets the perception of balance, the Seesaw Theory.

"You were famous and then I saw your seesaw move down, but now you're telling me that while it was moving down, you just *jumped off* that seesaw to another. And now that new seesaw is rising up, but not in the area of Fame again, but to a part of the sky that is Personal and Creative Satisfaction, WHAT THE FUCK ARE YOU DOING?" It fucks that theory right up.

Some of them, like you, maybe, you can see that seesaw jump as permission, or proof, or inspiration to jump off your own seesaw, when you start to see it fall down. To grab your own pot of popcorn off the stove when the popping starts to slow down, so it doesn't burn. To leave the party before the lights come on. Jump off your own seesaw onto a new one and see that new one rise up. Maybe some will see that. Like I said, maybe that person is you. But for the most part, for many people, it's just confounding, this seesaw jump, this refusal to play one of the Five Roles for Post-Fame Women. It makes them a little frustrated that you got out of your box; a little angry that you walked out of your neatly labeled category; a little irritated that with so many things in disarray in their own lives, maybe at least you were well-defined and not in disarray; you were in this box, with this nice label.

"A touchstone for a part in my life, a treasure trail sure to take me back to that part of me I found when you were 24, but goddammit. You're a disappointment. You jumped out. You're just as much a disaster as everything else in here, as everything else in my life. You were something else, something I could count on. Even in one of the Five Roles for Post-Fame Women, you would have been a comfort to me; a faded flower pressed between the pages of my heavy book of treasure trail touchstones. You're no help to me anymore. I'm done with you. I will rip you apart on Twitter now. Every chance I get. You're not giving me the seesaw perception of balance satisfaction. You jumped seesaws; I don't know what you're doing. You're confusing me. Get away from me. You're not playing the part. You're contributing to the disarray I already have in here, in my life. Just go."

MAGICIANS

Let's talk about "One-Hit Wonders." You've got this person, a performer, who skyrockets to Fame. I'm not talking about the slow burn to Fame that some performers absorb over time or even the rapid rise of someone on a hit TV series, I'm talking about the almost immediate, overnight launch into Fame that can happen to a newcomer in a film that shatters box office records or to a musician who creates and performs a song that not only grabs everyone's attention, but indelibly crystallizes a pop culture moment in society. Musicians Milli Vanilli, Vanilla Ice, a-ha, Toni Basil, Frankie Goes to Hollywood, Survivor, Baha Men, La Roux, LMFAO, you know the rest.

People mock them. The people who once danced like there was no tomorrow to their songs, who once turned up the volume every time their songs came on, "YOU GUYS! DO THE MACARENA!" They then started hearing the smooth jazz versions of those songs in elevators and doctors' offices, and they started to feel shame for liking something that now seemed so mainstream, so they began to push it away. From themselves, from their life.

"Oh my God, how embarrassing," they say when

a friend shows them the picture of the two of them wearing *Too Sexy for This Shirt* ensembles at a '90s concert. "How embarrassing! We were idiots."

They want so badly for it not to be true. For it not to be true that they liked a song, were bananas for a song, the one that their dentist now plays from the "easy listening" Pandora station she made, the one they hear while they get their teeth drilled. They mock those musicians because they don't want to be associated, because they are afraid of what others will now think of them.

OK. Let's talk about the performers. They are making their music, making their music, going along, and BAM. They land a huge hit. It's catchy, it appeals to an enormous number of people, and you watch the song climb the charts, break into the Top 100, the Top 50, the Top 10. Holy shit. The offers are pouring in. Talk shows, magazine profiles, "HOW DID THEY DO IT?!" They do the interviews, they perform on late-night talk shows. They are everywhere. They think, "OK, I'm in. I'm there." They think about what to do on their next album.

Now, I've told you enough about the expectation of someone who's reached great Fame. From a few pages ago. I've told you about the disappointment that the once very-famous see in the faces of the public when that Fame starts to fade. Imagine what it's like for these one-hit-wonder performers. Abject disdain from the public. You've got the disappointment that they're not as famous anymore and the desire to disassociate from their dentists' music choices. And those artists don't deserve that. In fact, I'm giving them a new name. "The Magicians." They get to be called the Magicians because what they did was to pull off something that almost never happens. Forget that they don't know how they did it or how to repeat that success. See? That doesn't matter. They grabbed that throbbing ember of Fame, like a hunk of the sun, even, and choked that down, with no water. You then saw the Supernova Fame light emanate from them and it was incredible. They never have to do it again to command respect. Ever.

Moon Zappa, who created the entire "Valley Girl" phenomenon with her hit song, in 1980's pop culture and beyond, never has to do another thing to command respect. She created the Valley Girl movement, which later extended from fashion to films, from scratch in her dad's recording studio. There in the Hollywood Hills, behind the garage, at the Zappa house. I was 16 at the time, living in the San Fernando Valley, and we'd never before referred to ourselves as "Valley Girls." We didn't act like that. We didn't talk like that (with the exception of saying "like" every third word). Moon took the speech pattern of the "Creekers" (the kids who lived in Topanga Canyon), the topics and wardrobe style of the JAPs (the Jewish American Princesses of the valley, namely Encino and Tarzana), and supercharged it all into that magnificent rap, "Valley Girl." She made the whole thing up. And yet, she tells me, people later brutalized her for not following it up with another cultural zeitgeist. People saying things to her like, "That's what you get for being a flash in the pan." Inexcusable.

Anyway, not to rant on about Moon, but if I ever see someone insult her in front of me, I'll take them down. Can you see how one would want the Fame back, just so they don't have to hear those kind of comments? So you have immunity again from seeing looks of disappointment in people's eyes and from hearing their disparaging comments?

UNSAFE

When the Fame started to fade, I felt physically unsafe. Sounds weird, I know. I didn't feel physically
unsafe when I was too famous, when everyone recognized me, but I did later, when only half of them
did. Fear of my physical safety. Weird, yeah. No one
was threatening me. Had no threats upon my life or
stalkers. Not like that stalker when I was 23 or so,
who traveled up to Berkeley where I was doing a
play. Who had been sniffing around *Family Ties* before, with all of us, trying to cozy up to Mike Fox and
Tina, mostly, and a little bit me. This guy followed
me up to Berkeley, I guess. Sent letters I didn't read,
but then had to. The ones that got your attention, if
you were famous, the ones where they talked about
"being together on the other side" and "finally being together forever." *Those were the ones,* you were
warned by Gavin DeBecker, the security advisor to
us all. Those were the ones you had to send to Gavin,
the ones from people who could descend upon you
like the fan who killed Rebecca Schaeffer. That. Had
some mutual friends there. "No way. Someone just
came to her house and stabbed her to death? Jesus.
Wow."

Home addresses deleted from utility bills, you had to. No Internet yet, to find out every bit of information about where you live (fucking dangerous collection of publicly accessed information, online now), but people who worked at the utilities had friends, those who might like you, who might like you too much. Maybe they'd pass on your info. Your electric bill, your phone bill, land line, your cable bill, your property tax bill, everything. Your address is on everything. Delete your home address. First thing Gavin told us. Get your home address off everything. Do not have your name and your address on the same document. Not deliveries from your talent agency, not your driver's license, not the birthday cards from your aunt. PO box for all of it. Get it off. Cameras for the front gate. Don't open the door. Packages, leave them there. Right there. I remember one of Mike Fox's assistants, she would take a Polaroid of every person who came to the house. A guest, a delivery person, the talent agency courier. She had to document them all.

So, this guy. Sniffing around Paramount Studios. How did he get on the lot? How did he get into our dressing room area? Shit, I don't know. Knew someone? I don't know. Follows me up to Berkeley. I'm doing a play. It's good. It's fine. Then some letters to the theater, from him. Photos of puppet shows. Do I know this guy? I mean, have I seen letters from him before? Have I ever sent letters from him to Gavin before? I don't know. I can't remember. I'm doing this play, I'm researching and learning my lines. Another envelope. Similar photos. Maybe a note. Shit. Is this problematic? I'm still recognized a lot. Is this concerning? These photos, this puppet show, some fucking metaphor? Shit. Move on from it. Then in town, I'm walking around in the town right there, near the theater.

"Justine!"

I almost never turn. Never turn to see who it is. Fans would call to me all the time.

"Justine!"

"Mallory!" One night, before, in LA. I'm 19, 20. In my house I bought so young. In there, by myself.

"MALLORY!" from a car passing by outside, the house close enough, against the street, to hear everything.

"MALLORY!" from a passing car, men. Maybe a truck. Maybe four of them piled into the back of a pickup truck like townies in a film. Townies with baseball bats who barrel down the street in the back of a pickup truck and knock down all the neighbors' mailboxes, especially the university professors', off their posts.

"MALLORY!" yelled as they passed my house. Oh fuck. Scared, because they know where I live. That thing. That one thing you did not want, that you tried to avoid, at all costs. Changed your address to the PO box for everywhere. Everything. You missed something, didn't change it somewhere, or someone saw you in the street, before, when you were walking in. The word is out. What if they tell others? What if they come back? When I'm outside, in my car, in my driveway. What if they come back. Me now, at the top of my stairs inside, by my bedroom door. Sitting, at the top. Sitting, listening, eyes looking. For what? I can't see out front from there, to the road. I don't know if they're coming back. They will try to look in, they'll try to break in, try to come in? Listening with my eyes, looking back and forth. Shit. I called my mom. I called the alarm company? Don't remember.

Can't call the cops. "They drove by, these guys. I guess there was more than one. They drove by my house and they screamed my character's name." No. What cop is going to listen to that shit. But I'm scared. I called my mom. Scared. What if they come back? I have no way to . . . They know my house.

So, in Berkeley, walking in the town near the theater and I hear my name. Never, almost never turn. UNLESS it sounded familiar. Unless it had that quality, that little tone that you use when you really know someone.

"Justine!"

For a split-second, I thought I heard that tone, I turn. Fatal—not fatal, but bad mistake. I turn and look, thinking it's someone who knows me. I turn and look for too long, for two whole seconds. I realize I don't know him and I realize right there, at the end of those two seconds, IT'S THAT GUY FROM PARAMOUNT. THE ONE WHO HAD BEEN SNIFF-ING AROUND MICHAEL AND TINA AND ME. THE ONE WHO CAROL HIMES, OUR LINE PRODUCER, BANNED FROM THE LOT. THAT GUY. Oh fuck.

I felt at that moment as if some cut had been made in reality and that there was no one who could help me. No cop—especially no cop—no person, no one around, no one. As if all of us, in that area, in the world, had been standing on a big piece of paper and in that instant, where I fatally—OK, not fatally, just bad—turned around to him, turned and looked for FAR too long. TWO WHOLE SECONDS. As if at that moment, because I looked, I let the paper be cut between us, between him and me. A cut in the pa-per, creating this slim canyon, where we could both fall. If he made a move toward me, he'd fall in and I would tumble after. If I didn't—OH MY FUCKING GOD, GET THE FUCK OUT OF THERE. HE COULD HAVE A GUN, A KNIFE, A—GET AWAY, RUN, GET OUT. The feeling that if I were to have looked and not turned back around, but looked for one more fraction of a second, I would have fallen into that cut-paper chasm and he would have jumped in there too, with me. And I don't know what would have happened af-ter that. It's just black and endless, no bottom, down in that dark place.

I don't remember what I did after that. Just got out, away from that situation. Got his information from Gavin, what Carol Himes had given Gavin, and gave pictures of him, the description, everything I then had, to the theater. OK. On the lookout for him. A precaution. No gun, no knife, we didn't see. He didn't say in his notes. Rehearse the play. Rehearse the play. Tech run-throughs. Rehearse.

Then, on the day of the opening. "Don't come to the theater. Not now."

The streets around the theater had been closed. Snipers were on the theater roof, and the roofs of neighboring buildings. What's going on? What happened? I'm not there. We're not there yet. It's early on the day of opening night. He has a gun. (Yes, he had a gun.) He had pulled it on himself. Was going to end it, take himself out. Was going to kill himself in the courtyard of the theater, because—or unless, I don't know—unless he and I "rekindled our relationship from when we were in Texas ten years ago." Me, at 23, trying to think if I met him when I worked in Texas before. (But that job was five years ago . . .) Me, trying to reason if I was somehow complicit here. WHAT THE FUCK. I was 23 or so. Ten years ago I was 13. I did not have a romantic relationship with this fucker when I was 13. He gets hauled off. The play opens. Fine.

I keep thinking when I'm standing onstage though, when I move down the aisle in that one scene, how easy it would be to shoot me right now, to take me so "we can be together forever." And who would be able to stop that? I get off-duty cops to follow me to and from the theater for the rest of the play's run. That's all I can do. The guy is put in jail. There could be copycats . . . I don't know. I just keep going, assuming, pretending I'll be OK.

Gavin had me talk to tennis champion Monica Seles after she was stabbed by that fan during a tennis match. I remember telling her that when I had my experience, I never felt more unprotected in my life. Not before then and not since. It's a fucked feeling. Someone, not rational, not reasonable, not sane, is after you. Will harm you in the name of "being together forever." They're signaling that you're going to die together. That's why it's the Gavin Alert, why you send him the letters that say that. It means they want to pull you down into that cut-paper canyon with them and fall forever into the darkness with no bottom. Gavin takes that seriously. You take that seriously, but others don't. That's right. Others do not. Because, you know, you're not-a-person. You're not real.

"They're just fans, relax, you signed up for this. C'mon, you're imagining things. You're famous. Your bundle of stuff makes everything all right. You're OK. You're overreacting. You're OK, famous person. They're your fans, they just love you. RELAX." Rebecca Schaeffer, John Lennon, Selena. It's real. They will kill you. If that's what's on their agenda, they will kill you.

* * *

But that was a specific instance, of feeling physically unsafe, of feeling the horror of that cut-paper fall into blackness. That wasn't at all how I felt most of the time when I was very famous. So, realizing I now felt physically unsafe as the Fame receded . . . I couldn't understand how or why I would feel that way. I was *less* of a target at this point. Less people recognized me, no stalker wanted me (that I knew of); they'd all moved on to people with more Fame. But no, I felt physically unsafe. Then I realized that being famous, being recognized, had given me immunity from harm. OK, forget the cut-paper-canyon-stalker thing; that was a specific instance. I mean that being recognized gave me a general immunity from harm. That I could step into any dangerous, or potentially dangerous, situation and know that at least one person, one face in that group, was going to wash over with recognition. One of those faces, dead set against admitting you to the group, is going to suddenly awaken in recognition of you. Their face is going to come alive and they are going to turn to the others in that group and vouch for you. They are going to turn to the others and say, "HEY! This is Justine Bateman! It's that girl! From *Family Ties*! That girl!" And the rest of the group will take you in. No questions asked, no needing to know anything about you, the real you. Just take you in. Accept you. TRUST YOU. Acceptance, protection, revealing of information, even.

Once I was on the corner of Gower and Santa Monica, not a great part of town, getting my car washed, getting gas, I don't know. A group of teenagers, young—13, 14, 15. They were tagging the bus as it approached the bus stop there. Tagging it, graffiti on it. I'm curious. Always.

"Hey, what are you guys writing?"

They turn away, not going to talk to me. I'm suspicious. Not just curious; bad, suspicious. White girl, early 20s. Only bad here. Turn away. Not going to talk with me. But, I see one guy, just one guy, it only takes one guy. A wash of recognition over his face.

"She's that girl! Hey, you know, *Family Ties*!" They all turn toward me. All speak now, all answer my questions now, give me information. All IN.

Even recently. A few years ago, doing research for a series I'm writing, about the orange-vested people cleaning the sides of the freeways in LA. What's that about? What are the details? Caltrans gives me permission to clean the side of the road with the rest of them, the ones who have to be there. I take someone's spot. Felt bad to take the spot of someone who has to work off these court-ordered hours. Stood in line in a dark parking lot at four in the morning, because you can't get a spot if you show up later. Only 15 spots per day, per lot. Have to get there early. Stood in line; was just going to observe, maybe ask a couple of questions. But recognition; they recognized me. I explain what I'm doing there.

And everybody, recognition, and being vouched for. Everyone opened up to me, told me. Confessed? Told me their stories, every single one of them. Am I a brilliant writer? They talk to me because of that? It was the Fame, not the writing, the Fame made them tell me everything.

This trust, this "We will never hurt you because you treasure-trailed right into that nice time I had, right now or years ago, that I had when I watched your show/film/play performance. You are in. We hold you in a place we have for Santa and leprechauns and Easter bunnies. You will never hurt me, you make me smile. We will let you in, you will never hurt me. You have delivered to me the lightness I needed. I will never hurt you." You are in.

They are not the lunatic break-into-Letterman's-house-kill-Rebecca-Schaeffer-send-puppet-show-photos-and-pull-a-gun-on-yourself-at-Justine-Bateman's-theater fans. They just recognize you, and you are IN.

Protected. You see what I'm talking about. Had it at 16. Strong Fame from 16 to 28, say. Over ten years strong, bright, can't-go-anywhere Fame. Then slightly faded, the Fame, for ten more years; still feeling that protection and not knowing it. Unusual. An unusually long time with a great deal of Fame. But, at the end there, where the Fame started to slide down uncontrollably. Sand-through-the-fingers Fame fade, slip. There, I started to feel afraid. Physical-safety fear and I couldn't understand why. It was that. That absence of the wash of recognition over people's faces where they'd vouch for you to everyone. That was going, gone. That was going, fading. Soon, I would be recognized by not even half of the people. Someday it would only be some, just a few. I would be on my own, physically. Would have to defend myself. Never learned that, didn't develop that. Never needed to, until now. No one to help, no one to recognize, no one to vouch for me, to tell everyone, "She's OK! She's that girl!" No embrace, no protection. So, I realized I was accustomed, didn't know any different. Had not known much else. For most of my life, I'd just known that protection feeling that flows from being recognized in potentially bad situations and being vouched for. And now that was going, soon to be gone. And it took me by surprise, this surprise feeling of being physically unsafe.

LEPER

There's another thing that happens when the Fame has faded, when it has descended in that sand-through-the-fingers way. It's rotten and uncomfortable. You're already getting some of those slightly disappointed looks when you go out, and you know that public-adulation part of your Fame reality has already being pulled out from under you. But then you feel it from others in the business, your contemporaries; that's the rotten and uncomfortable part. This was me, at a birthday party in LA, at a club where about half the people were well-known, famous. Me, then feeling them wanting to peel away from me. My Fame had been fading for a while. I had had the clothing company, had come back into the business and done a Showtime series and a few pilots. But, I don't want to make this about career. We're keeping the focus on Fame. Let's say I'm squarely, involuntarily in that frustrating "Are you still acting?" moment in public, with Fame.

It was around 2006/2007. So, my Fame is nothing like it once was, but I'm the same person. I still have the same talent and skills as before. Nothing should have changed between me and other actors,

performers, in my business, right? I go to this party,
I may have gone by myself, even. I know the birthday boy, and some of his friends, so I probably went
alone. I make conversation with a couple of people I
know and I meet a few new people. But, I notice that
the well-known people, the very well-known people,
the ones who have the level of Fame I had had not
long before, these people kind of lean away from me.
The polite, tight smiles when talking to me, as if I'm
somebody's cousin visiting from Ohio. Fucking really?
I mean, that "Wassup" between two equally famous
people, with the head nod across a crowded room, in
an airport, wherever. The "I know what you're going
through. I dig you. Wassup?" That was gone. That
was not being offered to me anymore, not at this
party, maybe not ever again. Fuck. Not that I was sad
that these famous-as-I-used-to-be people weren't
becoming my best friends. It was this feeling that I
was being regarded as a fucking LEPER. As if there
was some scent I was emitting, some toxin that
was warding off Fame and continuous employment.
As if getting near me would contaminate their still-
ascending Fame. Me. Justine Bateman. (Sure, call
me arrogant.) Such a shitty feeling.

In psychology they call this "stigmatization," the
roots of which are in "disease avoidance." An evo-
lutionary survival technique, sure: avoid those who
appear to be infected and survive. In doing this, we
create stigmas, a sort of shorthand for who to avoid,

only our brains often do not make the distinction between conditions that are contagious and those that are not.

On the one hand, I wanted to get the hell out of there and lick my wounds and carry on with my can't-get-traction-in-the-Fame-world life alone. On the other hand, I wanted to take hold of them and say, "Listen, stop with the fucking attitude. Look at me as the person I am, not by the measure of my current Fame. You're not going to fucking catch it." But hey, who knows how Fame works. Maybe you *can* catch "Faded Fame." I don't know. Fame is so mercurial. It was not something they were willing to fuck around with.

Now, here, you know what happens. When someone treats you, a whole collection of people treat you, a certain way, you have a choice. You can either reject this reality they're trying to spray on you and decide they're just a bunch of stupid children, or you can try to *make sense* of how they're treating you, how they are "right." The first choice has you making them wrong. The second choice, the leper choice, has you making *yourself* wrong. And what's the risk? The first choice, where they're wrong and you're right, where you recognize that they are trying to impose a reality on you because of their own fears and insecurities, leaves your self-esteem intact. But it also puts you out in the cold. You are now *not* part of their reality, because you won't play the part they have assigned you. You are separate, you are other, you are out. The second choice, the one where you are a leper, makes them right and you wrong. And what do you get from picking this choice? You get to participate in their world. Yeah, I know that sounds strange. If the only way you can participate in their world now is to play the part of the Faded Fame Leper, why would you want that? Well, ask any fat kid who ever let his seventh grade class mock him all year. At least that way they had "accepted" him, at least he was IN.

You, reading this book, in your living room, on the couch, by the window, maybe a cup of tea by your side. Or you, on an airplane, in the darkness, reading with the overhead light on, even though your seat-mate is trying to sleep. You may think that sounds bizarre, for me to have taken that second "leper choice" at the party, where I was wrong and they were "right," in order to feel part of their reality. But we do it all the time. In small ways, big ways, we all do it. And every time we tell ourselves it's harmless. Most of the time, we don't even realize we're doing it.

Maybe you are at a gathering of people who are a little fancier than you. Maybe those well-dressed moms at your kid's school or people at a rival company whom you see at every trade conference. Maybe it's the volleyball team you play against, from that school across town, the ones who always seem so above it all. These are people who react toward you as if you are lower or different or just something you're not. They are trying to impose a reality on you, see? They look down on you, maybe. They cast you as a character that's not you. And you choose. You make a choice to let them be wrong or to let them be right. If you decide they are wrong, you keep your self-esteem, but you lose the opportunity to "connect" with them. If you decide to make them "right," you feel like shit about yourself, but at least you have an invitation, almost, to be part of their world, because you're playing a part they have given you. You get to choose. Every single time.

That's what I did with the Gold Dress Episode and the Face Disaster. With the Gold Dress Episode, I decided that the "critics" were wrong about my dress, and that I was right about my dress being awesome. I picked *my* reality and I felt great as a result. In the Face Disaster, where I was ripped apart online for the appearance of my face, I decided that I was wrong and that the trolls were right about my face being a horrifying sight. I picked their "imposed reality" and I felt terrible for years as a result. It's not fucking worth it.

TANYA77

So there I am, for years and years, when the Fame was thick, on guard in the public, braced for anybody at all to come up to me, for who knows what reason. Watching how I act, what I wear, how I respond to people. Knowing that my reaction was going to be counted as my "official response." There was never ever a rehearsal to find out who you really were. Your response cannot be an experiment. It can't be a rehearsal. You get one take and it's final (and probably documented). You were always going out in this full-body costume, this dealing-with-the-public costume of behavior.

When the Fame had finally faded, I could start dealing with the public in a real way, an organic manner, the way I honestly wanted to respond. It was invigorating. It was in small ways, sure—with the drugstore cashier, with the car wash attendant. I was no longer bound to behaving self-consciously. Being famous for a long time leaves you with this vestige of people-pleasing, one that you can't shake off until the Fame really fades. You get stuck "being nice" everywhere you go, no matter the circumstances, no matter what the paparazzi are yelling at you. I had a reminder recently, of that. I was on my way to a meeting with a publisher, for this book, in fact. I was walking through 30 Rock in Manhattan, where NBC is based, to grab my book agent beforehand, and I happened to walk into the side entrance door of the building. I walked a few feet into the building, looked to my left, at the burgundy carpet runner against the wall, and I remembered the last time I had been in that exact spot. 1988, I was hosting *Saturday Night Live* and we'd just finished rehearsals for the day. Because the producers wanted everyone to be on the late schedule of Saturday's live performance, you worked late all the other days as well. It was two a.m. when I came down the elevator and started through that portion of the lobby to the side door where my car was waiting. 10 or 12 paparazzi were suddenly on me, there in that narrow part of the lobby. Look, this was unusual back then. You didn't have the photographers following your every move like you do now. The public noticed every move you made then, sure, but not the paparazzi. It was also a surprise to see them because it was two in the morning. Anyway, there they were, on me.

"Justine! Right here!" SNAP, SNap, snAP.

I'm stunned. I didn't expect to see them. I'm not prepared, hadn't expected it. It's late, I'm tired, I'm surprised. I push through. No physical contact, I just keep walking, I don't stop.

Then, suddenly, "WE MADE YOU! YOU'D BE NOTHING WITHOUT US!"

This is what one or two of them yell at me. Again, different time. More common now, sure, but back then, a little bit shocking. So, yeah, I was shocked, stunned. Wow. I get into the waiting car. Then, the self-analysis. Me, there in the back of the black town car, on my way back to the hotel. "Should I have waited? For them to take a picture? Should I have paused? Was I a bitch? Oh, God, please. Was I a bitch?" Assholes. I was 21. Hosting *Saturday Night Live* for the first time. Two o'clock in the morning and they ambushed me. And I'm worried if they think I'm a bitch. Assholes.

There's that attention, all the time for years, and you don't act like yourself in public, not really. It wasn't until my first Tumblr account in 2008 that I ever broadly behaved like myself in a public forum. I'm not talking about the small exchanges with cashiers and dance class teachers, I'm talking about publicly broadcasting who you really are, for all to see.

Fame had pretty well descended for me. I was primarily doing digital media and loving it. But for all of Fame's fading and my proximity to the Without of Fame, I still had not yet broadly, publicly let down my guard. So, I get on Tumblr and my friend Eric gives me a "starter list" of people to follow. Mark Lisanti, Alex Balk, Brett Dykes, TopherChris, etc. And I look at their posts. Holy shit. Editors, contributors to *Gawker, Defamer, Radar*, etc. Soon I added more.

Most of the then-small staff of Tumblr; Maloney and Karp; Molls and Anthony DeRosa, who would become a rising star in the political blogosphere and beyond; Steven Meiers, cultural anthropologist photographer extraordinaire; all of them. Satirical, funny, sarcastic, angry, political, biting. It was like falling into *Spy* magazine, my favorite magazine of all time. (By the way, landing the cover of *Spy* in 1988 and also being caricatured in *Mad* magazine in 1985 were the highlights of my Fame.)

So, there I was on Tumblr, following these wicked-smart, clever people, and me there under an alias. Yeah, yeah, sounds so dumb now. "I can be anyone online!" But, for anyone who was a known entity, who had been famous, who had been watched every day for years and years, this 2008 situation was a revelation. It was real freedom. To be able to express yourself, and to be in the company of this caliber of satire and cleverness. Expose your true personality so broadly with no ramifications, no blowback; it was something new. I had that for months too, before anyone figured out it was me, "Justine Bateman." But, by that time I had firmly established online relationships with a lot of these people. Them as themselves and me as myself, my *Tanya77* self. They knew me as the real me, and *then* knew I was, or had been, or still was, I didn't fucking know anymore, famous. In that order. The last time I had had that experience was in high school with my

Taft High School classmates, back when I got *Family Ties*. They were the last batch of people who had first known me as real me and then knew my Fame.

We're more savvy now. We might have nine Twitter accounts and three Facebook accounts, each with different personas, one for each of our interests. One for arguing politics, one for an adoration of film noir, and one that only your friends at the tennis club know is really you. This was before we became so matter-of-fact about the expressive freedom online. Maybe you can relate. It was still the beginning of social media. It was the glory days of Tumblr. We're talking pre-Yahoo-purchase Tumblr. It was tight. And to publicly interact with others as your true self, after having been too famous to ever touch that, was a revelation.

PHONE

You get used to people knowing your name when you're famous. You get used to people giving you access. You know that if you say your name over the phone, you will get that restaurant reservation, you will get that secretary to get her boss for you, you will get completely satisfying customer service. You just know. You get used to that. When Fame starts slipping away, that's one of the first ways you notice. Maybe there's a new maître d' at one of your regular restaurants and he doesn't know (how is that possible) your name. I can remember when that started happening.

Normally, you'd call and first thing out of your mouth was always, "Hey, this is Justine Bateman. Who's this?"

And they'd say their name, "Gina!"

"Hi, Gina. I was wondering if you have a table for four at eight tonight . . . Uh huh, in an hour . . . Yeah? Great. Thanks!" You'd say the name right up front so you could avoid the time it takes for this version:

"Hi, I'm calling to see if you have a table for four at eight."

"Tonight? You mean in an hour? I'm afraid we

are booked. The next availability we have is in a week. Would you like to make a reservation for next Thursday?"

"No thanks. Can I leave my name and number with you in case there's a cancellation tonight? I'm at 555-6273. Justine Bateman."

"OK, um . . . Oh, you know, I think we may have something. Can you hold on a minute?"

"Sure . . ."

"Hi, yeah, Justine? Why don't you come on in. At eight. It's no problem."

See? The first version is shorter.

So, I remember when the first version stopped working. It would work sometimes, but not all the time, which was awkward and it left me open to the hostess possibly treating me like shit.

"I'm afraid we don't have anything tonight."

"Do you have a waiting list?"

"Um, sure. What did you say your name was again? Can you spell that?"

Fuck that. I stopped using it. My name. Started making reservations under another name or using my name like any other name and expecting nothing. So, this is restaurants, fine. But, you really hate hearing this from people in your own business. When I started writing and producing, I was calling talent agents for actors for my projects. Even if the agent knew me, the assistant may not have. Agents' assistants are in the difficult situation of needing to know who their bosses do and do not want to talk to. This may not always be clear. Everyone and their brother are calling agents all the time, looking for access to their clients. The assistant will know the names of the agent's clients and those producers and directors the agent deals with regularly, but there are a lot of names the assisstant doesn't know. After all, many of these assistants just arrived from out of town and were not weaned on the pages of *Variety* and the *Hollywood Reporter*. So, it's understandable that they may not know my name or the names of others, but when you get the pauses and hesitation from them . . . yeah, it just feels like shit. You, entertainment veteran, getting a pause and a "Can you say the name again? I'll be sure to pass the message on . . ." It just feels like shit. Sure, your Fame has faded, but these encounters make you feel like you've been kicked out of the entertainment business altogether. You feel like some aspiring filmmaker from Madison, Wisconsin, who is trying to crowbar her way into Hollywood. Fuck.

You see it happen with security guards at the entrance gates of the studios too. You once knew many of them on sight. Or they recognized you right off the bat.

"Hey, Justine! Welcome back!" and all that. Yeah, that goes away. You transition from that to handing over your ID and them dutifully printing out your pass and telling you to go park in the far parking structure.

No more "Ms. Bateman, great to see you! You're going to Stage 4? Just take any spot there near the stage door."

OK, look. Someone might think, "Why am I reading this bullshit? Boo-hoo, she can't park steps from her destination anymore. Welcome to life. That's what it's like for the rest of us. Oh my God, what a baby." Sure, that's right. What a baby. What's the big deal to walk an extra five minutes to the audition or a meeting or the first day of shooting? Who cares? The thing I want to show you is that erosion of reality, that part of a famous person's reality.

What if you were a regular at the gym. You know the people there and they know you. You're a long-time regular customer. They stay open a little later for you sometimes, and when they get promotional gear, they toss you a T-shirt or a branded water bottle, because you're all pals. Now, let's say the owners sell to a big chain and the management changes. Almost all the employees are replaced. You still have your membership, you still go and work out, and maybe now even the locker rooms get a facelift by their new corporate owners. Great. But, you are no longer special. They don't give a shit how long you've been a member there. In fact, the gym gets higher fees from new members anyway, so it would be great, even, if you left that particular gym. Then they could bring in a new, higher-fee-paying member in your place. No more keeping the gym open late for you. No more promotional-product gifts. You try, though. You try to keep the persona you had in that place; the nice, chummy feeling you always had in there.

"You know Mayra . . ."

"Who's that? Mayra?"

"Oh, Mayra, the old manager."

"Mayra . . . sure."

"Mayra used to toss me a T-shirt when they'd get the new designs in. What do you guys think?" You're there, leaning on the counter casually, a half-smile on your face, trying to bring a fun, relaxed intimacy into the exchange.

"I'm sorry, sir. We can't do that. It's against policy."

They move off to sign up another new member and you remain there, a little surprised, a little startled. You, still leaning on the counter in your palsy-walsy way, your attempt to recreate that coziness you had with the last staff members, the pre–corporate own-ership staff members. And you feel ashamed. So, that's what it's like. When you have some reality to which you've grown accustomed pulled out from un-der you. That's what it's like.

Look, it's not a good idea to have it to begin with, this Fame-based measuring stick. Sure, we agree, but there's no way around it when you're famous. And when that measuring stick does start warping or becoming faint when the Fame starts to fade, you have to start slapping together a new way to measure your worth. Remember what I said before, about the safety deposit box and getting it out before the bank blows? That's what this is. You have to get that box out. Your self-esteem, your self-worth, your identity. Get it all out and start looking at it against a new structure, a new measure of worth. That way, when the bank goes or that measuring stick disappears completely, you are not left there with just a bloody stump of You. And you have to do this *as* you see the Fame fade. If you wait until the end, you will be in a lot of trouble; we established that. For every uncomfortable exchange with a restaurant hostess who either doesn't recognize your name, or doesn't want to, you have to figure out what you imagine is now being taken from you, what fear is making you uncomfortable, what button she's pushing in you. So for every moment in the public, where no attention is paid to you, you have to figure out why that hits you in your self-esteem solar plexus. For every success by another performer whom you thought had less Fame, and frankly less talent than you, you have to understand how that has anything to do with your own identity.

You have to hammer these things and not let up. You let up and you will be destroyed. You've heard the stories. Drugs, alcohol, self-destructive decisions, suicide. Hollywood history is littered with these stories. Many of those stories, those tragic endings, link back to this moment we're talking about, the

Descent. Disentangling who you are from the Fame itself. It's difficult to do. It takes diligence and attention. Separating your worth from Fame, when you've been very famous, is like removing the circulatory system from a human body. Just pulling it right out. A system that other systems had grown dependent on. Just pulling that right out. It's jarring, it hurts, and if you don't replace it, you're not going to make it.

So, that's what I did. I journaled and I talked. I wrote and I wrote and I talked and I talked and I got to the root fear, whatever it was, every single time I felt less-than. Every single time I felt bad about myself after going through a situation as utterly not-famous, or almost-not-famous, or I-don't-know-if-you-think-I'm-famous. Every single time. Getting used to Fame being sprayed upon you is very different than getting used to Fame being erased off you. More accurately, it takes a little while to get used to the imposed reality of Fame, but once you've absorbed that reality, it takes a long time for your system to adjust to the idea that it's gone. You can see how the "Justine Bateman looks like a sea hag now" and "You're a used-to-be" and "Shut up, you D-rate actress" garbage that you see online doesn't help at all. But, what it does give you is a multitude of opportunities to work that shit out. To write or talk and figure out why those situations or those comments pushed your buttons at all. What unreasonable fear, buried inside, caused you to get your button pushed? Why did you not just glance at that comment and move on? Why did it bother you? And when you do that work, get rid of as many "buttons" as possible, you get a new grid, your new internal measure of approval. And you know what happens then? You become bulletproof. Try it. If there's some button in you that anyone can push, something that's been pushed your whole life, try finding out what fear of yours is at the root of that. It's inevitably something irrational, but that's OK. Pull it out, don't judge it. Pull it out and expose it to the air. It will start to decay.

LOBSTER

OK, I feel like I can press into the Without now. I was a good little rowboat companion and I took you through the badlands of the Descent of Fame, even though I didn't plan on it. Me, scraped and bruised now, and poisoned a little bit, from walking through that. It's OK. It's a good bit of emotional vomiting. I know you'll be there, understanding this whole thing the next time you see someone come at me on Twitter or in their blog. You'll know they're just a malicious asshole. You'll know the whole story about what it's like in here.

The Without. Are you ever really without Fame, once you've had it? Isn't it more like a lobster trap? Something you think you can escape later, but realize you can't, once you're inside. Here's the picture. There are all these lobsters in their lobster traps. Some are shining and happy. These are the ones currently famous. They're having lunch on the deck of the yacht, upon the sea. Lying on a table sucking caviar through a straw with all the other party guests, or sitting on the edge of the hot tub (careful not to fall in), chatting with some girl about the opening of her "third eye" in Peru last summer. But, most of the lobsters in their lobster traps of Fame are down at the bottom of the sea, post-Fame, having fallen off the deck of "favor" during their Descent. Down in the sea where it's quiet and cold and dark. Where you can see the plankton in the water when you look up, when the thin shafts of light cut down, that far down, into the darkness. Spooky. That's what it would feel like if you didn't get your security deposit box out before the bank blew. If your self-esteem and your identity and your self-respect were taken out in the blast. Down, down at the bottom of wet blackness.

But, let's talk about another scenario. One where you *did* get your shit out before the blast, where you processed all the uncomfortable feelings as they happened. You're a lobster in a lobster trap, but you're not on the deck of the yacht nor down at the bottom of the sea, in the dark. You're instead walking around on shore, in that little seaside town there. And now you're just without Fame, but never able to go back to being completely unknown. Maybe you get recognized once a week, or once a month. Maybe people "know who you are" and don't say anything. You can't tell. You have some currency in the Fame account. Just a little. It might get you an extra bag of peanuts from an older flight attendant next time you're on a plane, but that's it. At least it feels like that's it.

Years ago, I started telling myself that I wasn't

famous. I repeated this over and over to myself. It just made it easier. It made it easier in those situations where in the past, you would naturally assume you'd be treated as famous. A fund-raiser, for example, where pictures are taken of actresses who don't seem that much more famous than you, and few, if any, pictures are actually taken of you. If I told myself that I wasn't famous, then experiences like that weren't so bad. Tell myself that and then do the writing to get rid of whatever lingering "button" was still there. But, hey! I wasn't even acting anymore anyway, right? Comparing apples and oranges. "I'm a writer, director, producer now. Behind the scenes now. Yeah, I'm not famous and who cares?"

So, this worked. It was a good method. When people did recognize me, it was more of a surprise to me than a thin representation of the recognition I used to have. In fact, I could even tackle the "Aren't you an actress?" question with "Oh, years ago!" and save myself from hearing the "Aren't you working on anything now?" follow-up question. If they pressed the issue, I could say I worked behind the camera now, and just shut down that whole line of inquiry. You know, it's like I said before, they don't want to hear about my writing or my recent UCLA degree or my producing or the new projects I'm directing. Many just want to hear about something that elicits the attention, or gets close to eliciting the attention, that *Family Ties* had. Even after I got into UCLA as a freshman at 46 to study computer science, people's reaction to that paled in comparison to the reaction to my appearance on the ABC TV series *Modern Family* later that year. I shot one day on it, enough to qualify for the union health insurance while I was in school. People's eyes would just light up when they realized it was me they'd seen in that episode. By this time I was so burrowed into my "I'm not famous" fur coat that I thought their reactions were bizarre. It was far more difficult to get into UCLA to study computer science than it was to say a few lines on camera. I found their reactions completely backward.

I gotta tell you, if you can get rid of all those buttons, post-Fame, then being in the Without is pure freedom. You are free to never people-please again. You can act however you want. You can truly not give a shit what people think of you, of how you dress, or what you say. What do you care? You have no Fame-dependent career on the line here. Pure freedom. You can even still use the Fame sometimes. When I was at UCLA, virtually none of my classmates knew who I was, but my professors did. And maybe that made my permission-to-enroll requests stand out in a sea of permission-to-enroll requests, because I never had a problem getting whatever classes I wanted. I paid for that Fame currency, for whatever I've got left. I paid for it for a long time. I've got a few coins left in the silk-lined pocket of this "I'm not

famous" fur coat and I will use them, when it works.
That's how I feel about that.

STARS

Interacting with famous people now takes on a new sheen in the Without. There don't seem to be any in-between reactions. Famous people either know and respect you or you get the cousin-from-Ohio treatment. The straight-arm, "I don't want to know you, I don't ever want to know you" treatment. You're not getting the leper treatment anymore. No, now it's just respect or it's shit. The respect is great. I love e-mailing, or DMing on Twitter, people whose work I respect. I never do it to get a response, but sometimes they will respond with a "Oh hell! I love your work too! We should do something together!" That's tight.

The flip side of that is a blank look and the condescending tone reserved for annoying fans. And maybe if you're an annoying fan, you don't notice, but I notice, because I USED TO BE ON THE OTHER SIDE OF THAT. Not that I spoke condescendingly to people back then, but I know what it's like to be on the other side and to be in a situation that would warrant that reaction. I also know the body language of a famous person who's bulldozing through. The absence of eye contact, the furtive looks around themselves, to avoid any approaching fans. I get it; I've been there. So, it's really weird when someone does it to you, having been famous before.

I once saw actor Aaron Eckhart coming out of Pottery Barn a couple of years ago. Now, this is not a dig on Eckhart. This is about me, not him. I see him come out of the store as I'm walking toward it. We meet eyes for a second. I realize it's him and my instinct is to, I don't know, say "Hi." I liked his work a lot, so I fell into that well-worn "Wassup" mode for a moment, even though I was squarely in the Without of Fame. While I was thinking about that, I could see that he had very quickly looked away from me, with that, "Oh shit, I just met eyes with someone; they're going to try to talk to me" look. BULLDOZE. BULL-DOZE, BULLDOZE.

And he rushed past me. I don't fault him. He doesn't need to know who I am, but sure, it felt like shit, because I was suddenly cast in the cousin-from-Ohio role. I was the cousin-from-Ohio who came to Los Angeles to see movie stars.

Sometimes you know the celebrity a little, but you don't want to see that dreadful forgetfulness look on their face here in the Without, so you don't say anything. Maybe I remember meeting them better than they remember meeting me, so I don't want to risk it. I even resort to the old, "Hey! It's Justine!" when I'm standing right in front of those I know fairly well. Just to jog their memory, so I don't have to see them trying to put a face and a name together. Maybe it's ridiculous for me to do that, but I don't feel like taking the chance. Hell, I can remember all kinds of people coming up to me when I was very famous and trying to get me to remember meeting them before.

In the beginning of my Fame, they'd say, accusingly, "You don't remember me," or, "Oh, we've met before" (which launched my other, almost-patented "It's nice to *see* you" when being introduced to someone, instead of the traditional "Nice to meet you"). So, they'd say this to me, and me, being young at the time, I went ahead and felt ashamed that I didn't, in fact, know them. Later in the Fame, I would flat out ask them, partly because I was curious where we'd actually met, and partly because I thought they were full of shit.

There was one guy, I must have been late 20s, one guy responded with a vague, "Remember? New York?" I said that New York was a big place where I'd spent a lot of time (not to mention having been born there). Then, for "clarity," he adds, "New Year's Eve?" Yes, now I see it. You mention the busiest town in the country, on the craziest night of the year. So, no. I don't remember you. We have never met before.

Not too long ago, I was leaving a gated community after visiting a friend. On the way to the front gate, I see musician Gwen Stefani pushing a stroller. I know her a little bit, so I was going to say "Hi." But, as my car gets closer, I notice that she has that avoidance body language and that furtive look. She has every right to it. She's in her private community, walking her baby, and she probably tenses up every time she hears a car come up the street. Hell, I would. Now, maybe this sounds stupid, because if I had said, "Hi," that tense body language would have probably slid aside and we would have had a nice exchange, but I drove past. I didn't want to take the chance that she'd forgotten when we talked at her house party, or when she'd given me some backstage passes to her concert. I just didn't want to risk being looked at as the cousin-from-Ohio. I just couldn't risk getting that awful look. (Gwen, if you're reading this, I swear I'll stop and say "Hi" next time.) (And some cousin from Ohio is freaking out right now. It's just some state I picked. Nothing personal.)

There's this other time that sticks with me. I don't know if I was in the Descent yet, maybe just the Slide, but I'm in a movie theater, there by myself. I notice that a very famous actress is sitting in the row in front of me with her friend. She's sitting just a few seats over in the row in front of me, and this is a pretty big "sighting." I lurch forward (really, I do) and tap her on the shoulder.

"I love your work," in a loud whisper.

"Thank you," she smiles back.

Now, I don't like her work at all. So why did I do that weird thing? Why didn't I just sit there and wait for the movie to start and watch the film and then leave and go home? What was with the sycophantic "I love your work" from me? I sat back in my seat, amazed at myself, at my lurching, my shoulder-tapping. I could have sworn, even, that the actress's friend had given me a look, like she knew I was full of shit or something. A knowingness that I was fully prepared for her to call me on if we ever crossed paths again in town. Yeah, what the hell was that about? Sure, regardless of my opinion of her work, she was still spectacularly famous. I guess I did that thing that we do sometimes, when we're face to face with Fame. I guess I just reached out compulsively, because it was there, right in front of me.

I'm not the only one. It happens. It happens. Writer/actor Buck Henry told me about this time he was at one of actress/producer Colleen Camp's famed parties at the Sunset Tower. Lots of actors and actresses there. He's talking, chatting, and then finds himself face to face with a very tall, very famous blonde. He's introduced. He says that a few minutes later, he felt like he was "having an out-of-body experience." He was there, outside of himself, watching himself, prattling on and on with this woman who didn't know who Buck was. Seems impossible. The prolific Buck Henry (*Saturday Night Live, The Graduate, Catch-22, What's Up Doc?, The Man Who Fell to Earth, Heaven Can Wait, Defending Your Life, The Player, etc.*)? Impossible. So there he is talking, can't stop talking to her. Outside himself, watching himself go on and on to her. Her, not knowing who he was, annoyed maybe that he was talking to her. Feels like shit. I know the feeling. Buck said it pissed him off that he couldn't stop talking. For the next 48 hours he was pissed at himself for that.

I'll tell you about this other "encounter." This is me, in the Without. I'm in a private restaurant/club. It's daytime, and I think I'm probably working on this book, ironically. Probably transcribing the hours and hours of interviews I did with other famous people. Anyway, I'm at this place where a fair amount of famous people spend time. People are working on their laptops or having lunch or coffee. There are dining room tables and coffee tables and chairs and couches. The place is full, as usual. I get up at one point to go to the bathroom or something, and I start to navigate around the tables and couches. I turn one way and then another until I'm near a couch. I turn to my right to go around a table, but someone is coming that way, so I turn back to my left to walk past the back of the couch. Standing there now is a guy, a somewhat-known actor. I assume he's going to step aside so I can move past. That's what a normal person would do. But, that doesn't happen. He locks eyes with me and then perches on the back of the couch. He extends his long legs to block my path, and folds his arms, and looks at me, as if to say, "Do you think you can get past this?" Are you fucking kidding me? And no, he wasn't smiling. This was not a flirtation or a "fun game."

Now, you don't know me, but I'll tell you. If this had been in a normal situation, I would have had a different response. If I had not been in this particular restaurant/club, and if this had been a regular guy and not a somewhat-known actor, I would have said, "Are you fucking kidding me? Move." But, Jesus Christ, I'm in the Without and he, maybe not so much, or at least he doesn't seem to think he is, and it would have been a fucking scene had I said something. And honestly, if I were more famous at the time, he would have never tried that shit on me. That's the fucked-up part. So, I turned around and wound my way back through, to find another route to the bathroom. Yeah, that was a weird one. I wasn't willing to have my Fame temperature taken there in the middle of that place, if he, deciding he's more famous than me, started filling the room with an embarrassing conflict. He had his posse with him. I had none. Sounds lame, maybe, but that's what you get sometimes, in the Without.

PALLET

The Without is where you get to take that little pallet of dirt, with the core seeds you started with and the exotic seeds you collected from faraway lands, the plants that took root and the plants that died away, and carry it off the ship. You say goodbye to Captain Fame. You step onto the mainland and you dig all the plants out of that pallet and put them in the ground, there in the earth, in your plot of land. You get to dump out all the soil with the seeds that haven't yet burst forth and press it all into your large earthbound plot of land. In some ways, you're picking up where you left off, before you became famous. In other ways, you're beyond that, because you're expanding all the plants, exotic and otherwise, that you collected along the way. The exotic ones are the truly great ones to expand. Most of those plants never make it back to the mainland. Most of the time they are lost at sea, floating away from some Fame ship that's been wrecked on the jagged rocks of despair, drugs, alcohol, and suicide. In those cases, these exotic plants float away on their pallets until they burn up in the sun, bobbing up and down on the waves, there with no distilled water to refresh them. Bobbing up and down in the incessant sun, while that lobster in its lobster trap sinks slowly to the bottom of the sea.

Expanding those exotic plants on the mainland is unique. And everybody knows it. So, yeah, Fame is a lobster trap. And Fame is not real, but society won't let it go. So, maybe you'll see me later, walking around the seaside town. Me, a cute lobster, in a lobster trap, with an exotic flower tucked behind one of my ears that "stick out too much," and a locket around my neck with a tiny picture of Captain Fame. Say "Hello," and marvel at my stunning face. When we're done talking, I hope you'll tell me, "It's nice to *have* met you."

REAL

So, I think that's it. That's what I wanted to tell you about Fame. That's what I remember, and those are my theories. Maybe now you can reject someone's imposed reality on you, if you inhaled the self-help moments here. Maybe now you'll see the red carpet, pre–awards show experience on TV with different eyes. Maybe now you'll have more compassion for your once-favorite film star. But, maybe some people won't. Maybe they'll still see anyone with Fame as the enemy—selfish and privileged, rich and uncaring, childish and stupid. If so, I guess we'll see those people on Twitter, ripping us a new one. I hope not. If I've turned one hater here, with this book, it will have been worth it. Me, crawling through the thorny bush of the Slide and the Descent, having told you my loathing of memoirs and possibly insulting my friends.

I hope you can see that the bestowing of Fame is not some ultimate signal of God's approval, or anything like that. It's just this strange, societally made structure we keep alive so that we can have the hope that things can change, can get better for us. The Fame structure in our society is really just us imposing our self-will, trying to force some "nice provision" for ourselves. It's an indication that we, in fact, don't trust God (or the universe, or the sun, or whatever you want) to make things better for us, such that we set up this immense Fame game board to insure that there will be a guaranteed chance, at least, of us landing on a square and climbing a ladder to Fame, to "ultimate favor." Well, that's all bullshit. So, don't feel bad if you never "get famous." Don't freak out if you have less than 300 Twitter followers. It doesn't fucking matter.

Here's the point I want to make about the pursuit of Fame; it's something I hope can be absorbed, really seep into society. The pursuit of Fame—I'm not talking about the Fame that is sprayed on you because you are just doing your work—the *pursuit* of Fame will shut your true self off. Or, as Mike Fox says, "If Fame is the horse that leads the cart, you're never going to change, and you're going to be looking up an asshole that's going to dump shit on you every once in a while." If you are looking to be famous, at any cost, for any reason, then you are only allowing a shell of yourself. It's harsh, I know, what I just said. But, it's true. If you are reading this right now, and that is true for you, I'm here to tell you that YOU ARE REALLY INTERESTING AND YOU NEED TO LET THAT FLAG FLY. There is nothing interesting about pursuing Fame. It will not fix your problems. It will not bring you that bundle of nice things, not in the right way. To pursue Fame, you must cut off, you must not pay attention to, any of the things you are truly good at.

Here's what I'm saying: You have a basket of skills and talents that no one else has. You are born with them. Your talent may be working with the elderly. You're really good at it; it brings you pleasure, a feeling of accomplishment, but you know you are never going to be famous doing it. So maybe you hide that gift. You shove it down in the bottom of the laundry bag, down under last week's socks, because you want to pursue something that everyone, that all others, deem "important." And like we've established, society thinks that Fame is the top of the line. So, you go after it. And you shut off your gift. And so, it is lost to us, it is lost to our society, your gift with the elderly, say. Think about it. How many people, right now, are shutting off gifts for our current society because they are instead pursuing Fame. We are missing out. Our society is not as rich because of it. We have put such a false, bloated value on Fame that our entire society is missing out of the true gifts and talents of many. If this is you, please let us see you. We need you. Society is not what was intended without you letting us see who you really are. Our society right now assumes we should feel shame about positions that are not "famous." That is ridiculous and I hope you'll press against it.

I'm not going to blow smoke up your ass. I'm not

going to tell you, "You are a shining star, just as you are!" Shit, that's the basis of the reality show cancer in our country. No, you have to work at it. You have to take those skills and talents and you have to work them and you have to have the guts to let everyone see what you're good at. You have to fight that voice, either in your head or coming out of someone's mouth, that tells you those skills and talents "just aren't enough." Fight it, because you know they're full of shit. Refuse the imposed reality they're trying to spray onto you. They're only telling you what they tell themselves. What they're saying isn't real. But, you are real and your skills and talents are real. Stand up and be willing to feel alone; the feeling won't last long, there will be others there. Get fearless and get bulletproof. You can do it.

NOW

Let's get out of the rowboat. Just sit on the riverbank with me now. That emotional time travel is done. I'm glad I worked all that out with you. Let's just be here now. I have a fondness for the Fame, for what it was, for the little I have now. It's a kind of identifier. Sometimes that identifier is a target, sometimes it's just a way for people who like your work to pick you out of a crowd. As far as the big Fame I had before, like anything in our past, when you shake all the emotions out of it, you just see the good stuff.

It's funny, to be on the outside of the frenzy of Fame, to look at it from over here now. I was at the Toronto Film Festival recently. I was there as a writer/ director, with a film in the festival. An honor, a very public acknowledgment of what I now do professionally. So there I am, walking around town one night with one of my actors, Rob Benedict, and my manager, Larry Hummel. We're heading to a few parties and we come to a point where the sidewalk is completely clogged. The cause? People packed behind a barricade, craning their necks for a glimpse of the actors entering the theater for their film's premiere. I don't hold that against any of them in the crowd. It's interesting to have a bunch of your favorite actors in your town, all at once. It's interesting and people want to check it out. You could feel it, though, that "thing." That heightened anticipation, verging on mild hysteria. It's like a charge in the air. Like we're all suddenly in some giant MRI and the air is filled with electricity and a billion protons are aligned in the fans' bodies, there at the barricades. Each with his phone in one hand, ready to snap whatever faraway-celebrity-blur can be captured at this distance, their feet stubbornly planted until that shot is achieved. I don't blame the fans, but it was curious to watch, to be instead over here. For me to not only lack that Fame, that thing that elicits a frenzy that can't be seen past, but to also lack the concern with that absence. Knowing that the Fame I had before had to die in order for anything new to take its place.

And all the work I've done, with the writing and the talking, the getting-my-stuff-out-before-the-bank-blew, got me to the place where I could stand there, in that crowd of Toronto fans, and simply take notice. It got me to a place where I could be at those parties later that night, where the actors at the festival have more heat on them than almost all the filmmakers, and be fine, be amused. To only take passing notice of the Fame temperature being taken when the photographers came through, as they snapped photos of the actors near me, but not me. To be unconcerned with that Fame energy, and instead to relish the new track of notoriety I'm currently on as a filmmaker. To be walking down the street the next day and have someone stop me because they liked the film short I had at the festival, to have that kind of identifier, absent of the frenzy, to have renown and not FAME. And, further, to want the notoriety only in as much as it helps my filmmaking agenda; to help financiers, actors, etc., feel comfortable jumping into my projects. To help audiences decide to see my films, to help readers, like you, decide to dive into this book with me.

So what is Fame, in its purest sense? Apart from the societally made structure, the one we made up? The sheath we place on others, the machine we keep healthy in the hopes we might someday benefit from it? No, what is that intangible energy? I told you that on the last page we'd probably have an answer. What do you think? That ephemeral something that fills the air when the famous walk into a room.

It's something like projected love and intimacy, isn't it? As if to say, "I heard your music / saw your TV show / watched your film. I opened myself up to you then, I opened a vulnerable part in myself and I let you in. You, some artist I don't know, but someone who's also being vulnerable through your music, in your acting. You and me, meeting in that place. I let you in and we felt safe. So, I see you later, I see you on the street, I see you walk into a restaurant. You don't know. You don't know what we shared. And it's not crazy. I know we've never met, but there's something in my spirit that met you, before. Something that wants to fly out of me and meet you again, in that vulnerable place where we felt safe. And I'm not in control of it."

That's the best part of Fame. That creative identifier. I feel it too, when I see writers or directors I really like. The rest of Fame is the Chutes and Ladders game, really. Something fueled by fear and resentment and feelings of not-being-taken-care-of. The setting up of that game board in society, the steady diet of "They're just like us" photos of food spilling out of actors' mouths. The consequent harassment of them online. That's wholly something else and we may never be rid of it. We may never be able to shrink the size of that game board, but we can goddamn know the difference between the Fame borne out of love and the Fame borne out of hate and fear. And we can look past either one and we can be the type of people who don't seek it, people who don't hold Fame up as the apex of human existence. We can instead focus on and value our own basket of skills and talents.

Seriously, I can't wait to see what you do with yours.

Acknowledgments

I am grateful to the following people for their help in the writing of this book: Amy Scheibe, for showing this new puppy the publishing world; Holiday Reinhorn, for sharing your friendship and your publishing world experience; Seana Kofoed, for always being available to read my work and giving me your invaluable feedback; Judah Friedlander, for the introduction and the advice; Anthony Arnove, for not thinking like everyone else; Johnny Temple, for risking the more complex road; Buck Henry, Michael J. Fox, Cam Neely, Danny McBride, David Duchovny, Dylan Lauren, Elizabeth Much, Jason Bateman, Amanda Anka, Keith Rivers, Lea Thompson, Lesley Ann Warren, Mayim Bialik, Moon Zappa, Nancy Allen, Peter Bogdanovich, Treat Williams, and William Mapother—for sharing your time and insights.

Thank you to the photographers and publications that granted me reprint permission, for your generosity and help, especially Diane Nelson, Wendi Cassuto, Eva Sjoberg, Dawn Airey, and Carrie Byrne Putelo.

Thank you to Hunter S. Thompson, Herman Melville, Michael Herr, Walt Whitman, and David Mamet, for spewing your words on the page in a visceral manner and confounding English grammar instructors; Dr. Terri Anderson for the introduction to all the sociology masters; and Professor Marcus Anthony Hunter, for the friendship and the feedback.

Thanks to Tracey Jacobs, for sending me out to the *Family Ties* audition when you weren't supposed to; Donald De Line, for being the perfect casting gatekeeper; Gary David Goldberg, for bringing me into the nest that I had no idea I needed to survive; Nanci Ryder, for navigating the Fame waters for me when the rapids roared the loudest; Shelly Morita, for being in that boat with me when Fame was the thickest; Mike Fox, for being someone whose Fame footsteps I always felt I could safely follow behind; Rich Wilson, Pilar Calandra, Brooke Asher, Alan Sereboff, Aimee Graham, and Kelly Cutrone (and Deborah and Linda), for listening to me process everything over the years; my Topanga friends, for talking me out of throwing away my boxes of press clippings twenty years ago; G.J., for the wisdom and the magic.

Lastly, thanks to Duke and Gianetta, for your love, patience, and understanding; and to Marty, for your love, patience, and support, especially when it seemed confusing, and for being solid gold, always.